ALSO BY *ERNEST LOCKRIDGE*

Novels

Hartspring Blows His Mind

Prince Elmo's Fire

Flying Elbows

Literary Criticism

Twentieth-Century Interpretations of
The Great Gatsby

Memoir

*Travels with Ernest (*with Laurel Richardson*)*

SKELETON KEY
TO THE SUICIDE OF
MY FATHER, ROSS LOCKRIDGE, JR.,
AUTHOR OF *RAINTREE COUNTY*

For Jeredith
with affection,

Ernest

SKELETON KEY
to the
Suicide
of my
Father
ROSS LOCKRIDGE, JR.
AUTHOR OF *RAINTREE COUNTY*

ERNEST LOCKRIDGE

ΓΛΟΒΑΛ ΕΝΤΕΡΠΡΙΣΕΣ

2011

ISBN-13: 978-1460909768

ISBN-10: 1460909763

Second Edition

Website: www.ernestlockridge.net
Cover Design: Vincent
Cover Art: "Convergence," Acrylic on Canvas. Ernest
Lockridge, artist

"THE TRUTH DOES NOT CHANGE ACCORDING TO OUR ABILITY TO STOMACH IT." Flannery O'Connor.

"IF YOU DON'T LOOK FACTS IN THE FACE, THEY HAVE A WAY OF STABBING YOU IN THE BACK." Winston Churchill

ERNEST LOCKRIDGE, Yale Ph.D. 1963

1966--Assistant Professor, Yale University

ROSS LOCKRIDGE, Jr.

April 25, 1914-March 6, 1948

Dad called this his "*Raintree County* Look."

"All happy families resemble one another; every unhappy family is unhappy in its own fashion." **Tolstoy**

"Pity me not, but lend thy serious hearing to what I shall unfold." **Hamlet's Father**

"Listen with the trust you accord the batterer, the rapist, the assassin, to any mere mortal who admonishes you to 'turn the other cheek.'" **Pere Nabri**

"If I am not for myself, who will be? If I am only for myself, who am I? If not now, when?" **Rabbi Hillel**

"AS FOR THE EVIL, as for those who lose their grasp on the stuff of life, who become unable to cope with their world, are they to blame, or are they not also the victims of long circumstance?" Suicide Note, **Ross Lockridge Jr., March 6, 1948**

"As for the miracle of being--it is of course a miracle, but it is not necessarily a good miracle." **Suicide Note**

"Raintree County **is an epic novel of heroic proportions. John Wickliff Shawnessy, its hero, is the epitome of the place and period in which he lived, 19ᵗʰ-century America, a rural land of vernal women, of farmers, gamblers, wanderers, soldiers, orators, poets, and simple scholars.**

"Here on the banks of the Shawmucky River which wove its primitive course through Raintree County in Indiana, in the heart of America, young Johnny Shawnessy studied the classics—Homer and Virgil--in languages which had ceased to be the speech of living men, but which had once been, like Johnny's American language, the expression of freedom—the birth-cry of new-born republics. And here, too, in Raintree County were a young republic, shining waters, and much sunshine, and a young worshiper of the earth.

"Throughout his eventful life, J.W. Shawnessy would feel these ancient rhythms and follow classic patterns. He was the man of his century, which means he was all the men of his century. He fought in our bloodiest war, ran a political marathon, sought the meaning of a great city, and found the secret of existence as Mr. John Shawnessy, principal of the local school, who loved his wife and children, wrote poetry, and argued with his cynical friend, Professor Jerusalem Webster Stiles.

"*Raintree County* is written by a modern for moderns, but the prevailing mood is that of the century described. Ross Lockridge, Jr., tells his story through the device of a single day embedded with flashbacks. During this epic day, Mr. Shawnessy moves through a stream of past, present, and symbolic events. The day is July 4th, 1892—a glorious 19th-century Fourth, complete with flags, political celebrities, firecrackers, band music, revival meetings, and the G.A.R. parade.

"Though based on broad historical research, *Raintree County* is not an historical novel. Indeed, it evades definition, for it attempts no less than a complete embodiment of the American Myth."

"*In April of 1948, Ross Lockridge, Jr., carried* Raintree County *to the offices of Houghton-Mifflin in a suitcase. The manuscript, weighing 20 pounds, was piled on a table in an antechamber, where the author and an editor sat peering at each other over and around this Matterhorn of literature. In a few weeks, the manuscript was accepted and a contract signed. Still to come were the Metro-Goldwyn-Mayer Novel award and other successes for the Indiana writer's first novel. The contract, however, was the first tangible reward of a determination by Lockridge at the age of seven to be a writer.*

"Born in Bloomington, Indiana, on April, 25, 1914, Lockridge spent his formative years in Indiana. His father, Ross Lockridge, Sr., introduced him to history, the public schools to poetry, shorthand, and typing, and college—Indiana University and later The Sorbonne—to intellectual, literary, and artistic trends. Thus forearmed, Ross Lockridge, Jr., began teaching at Indiana University, working for an advanced degree, and writing. In 1940, he moved to Harvard on a scholarship and then accepted a teaching post at Simmons College in Boston. He remained there from 1941-1946, until his novel was written in its first complete draft—a task which required six years of research, writing and revision.

"Lockridge was married to Vernice Baker of Bloomington, Indiana, in 1937 and has four children—Ernest, Larry, Jeanne and Ross III. Through all the vicissitudes of residence and travel the Lockridges have considered Bloomington their home town.

"Soon after the publication of Raintree County, *its author, exhausted from years of labor, tragically took his own life."*

From the DUST JACKET, *Raintree County*

I

AN AMERICAN TRAGEDY

WHY did my brilliant father Ross Lockridge Jr. execute himself at 33, March 6, 1948, while his first novel, *Raintree County,* was *the number one The New York Times* Bestseller?

 Further, *Raintree County* had won the Inaugural Metro Goldwyn Mayer Novel Award, which included a nation-wide publicity blitz, plus the proverbial "pot of gold at the end of the rainbow." It had been the Book-of-the-Month Club's Main Selection of January, 1948. A lengthy excerpt had appeared in *Life Magazine*—America's premier organ of popular culture in the 1940s--which hitherto had not published fiction. *Reader's Digest* was publishing a condensed version. Critics and readers alike considered Dad's first novel, a labor of years, among the top contenders for that mythical *numero uno*, "The Great American Novel!"

This waste of a precious life and incalculable loss to literature bodies forth a murder-mystery that for six decades has extruded a slow crawl of platitudes: Dad was "worn out"; was unable to immediately begin a second novel and therefore believed himself to be "written out"; was destroyed by "the bitch-goddess Success"; was betrayed by a greedy publisher, a book club, by Hollywood; was unloved by his mother; was burdened with "patricidal guilt" for besting his father in the "Fame-Game"--*ad nauseam*. Not to mention Epistemology 101 and its soggy taboo: "Oh, my, we simply can never know even why we ourselves do the things we do, let alone another human being. Why bother?"

The ordeals that marred the publication of *Raintree County* are grossly disproportionate to the prodigious success in which my father should have been reveling. He had suffered setbacks before—some of them extreme—only to bounce back, stalwart in spirit and even more robust in resolve.

For, even as he was executing himself my father was experiencing success beyond the greatest of great expectations. Within the space of a few brief months Dame Fortune had transported him from poverty to wealth. Except for a *New Yorker* review notable for its gleeful Sadism, *Raintree County* was being praised throughout the land as the novel of the year, decade, Century, by far the most significant novel since World War II. My father died in full knowledge that his life, viewed from the street, had exceeded all but the most extravagant of human dreams.

Yet he left behind no last will and testament, no personal note of farewell--only four children, nine, five, four and two years old, and a lovely widow who worshiped the ground he walked on and whose 34th birthday was less than two weeks away. The afternoon of March 6, 1948, Dad borrowed the Electrolux hose with which his parents asphyxiated moles, and that night in our back-alley garage he taped the hose to the exhaust of our new Kaiser, locked the garage door, left the engine running, ran the hose through the rear window, crawled into the back seat, and--mere feet from the bosom of his loving family--died a squalid, lonely death.

This book holds the Skeleton Key to The Riddle of *Raintree County*. I have written it less from choice than out of an obligation to history and to truth.

Squeamishness and Mendacity, blood-brothers, go hand in hand. Miss Manners plays no part in this tragedy. Truth is not subject to etiquette or "taste," and it is precisely *because* the truth about my father's brief, terrible life and his forlorn death is unspeakable that the truth demands to be told.

Ernest Lockridge

II

MY PARENTS

Vernice Baker Lockridge and Ross Lockridge Jr.

Manistee, Michigan, late summer 1947. Mom hoped having their portraits taken might "make him feel better." She dates his "breakdown" as occurring "on or about Oct. 21, 1947."

III

LIKE ANY OTHER SUNNY DAY AT THE LAKESIDE

The "Old Folks"--"Grandpa" Ross Lockridge, Sr., and "Grandma" Elsie Shockley Lockridge--visit us in Manistee, renting a bungalow down the street from ours, late October, 1946.

That's me, 7, trying to tear myself loose from Grandpa Lockridge's grubby paws.

Dad shot the snapshot.

I traced the photograph on its backside. The little *jeu d'esprit* earned me my very own set of Sargent Oil Paints in the brown cardboard box for my 8th birthday that November 28:

Unmediated image of how I felt.

IV

DAD AND MARY JANE WARD, LITERARY COUSINS

Famous Authors of *Raintree County* & *The Snake Pit*
Manistee, Michigan, 1946

V

TYRANT AND TYRO

"Any design my captious fancy takes is as my natural food."
Shelley, *The Cenci*

1923--Ross, Sr., age 46; Ross, Jr., age 9.

"No one blames the child of less than ten for the errors of his personality." Suicide Note

VI

HOUSE OF HORRORS

Murmuring Maples, where my father, age 10, moved with his family, bears an unnerving resemblance to the Bates Home in "PSYCHO." "The Sun Room," which Ross Lockridge, Jr., shared with his father, Ross Lockridge, Sr., lies to the dwelling's rear.

VII

SMALL SACRIFICES

"I will make his youth the sepulchre of hope."
Shelley, *The Cenci*

Dad's older brothers Shockley (4) and Bruce (5)

Again and again, Bruce Lockridge had proven himself to be utterly incapable of swimming. Several times he had failed the swimming Merit Badge test to become an Eagle Scout. He could not even float. He would sink like lead. After being rescued from a stone quarry, Bruce challenged his mother to a breath-holding contest (he won). The next day, June 28, 1919, Bruce raced far out ahead of two friends into a rugged stretch of the St. Joseph's River near Fort Wayne, Indiana, and drowned. Bruce, 16, had just graduated from high school. My father was 5. The drowning was reported as "a tragic accident."

Shockley matriculated into Indiana University at 15 and promptly drowned himself in alcohol. Sheer intellectual brilliance kept him more or less afloat until, at 40, he joined A.A.

VIII

"SOME LIVES SEEM FORTUNATE"
Suicide Note

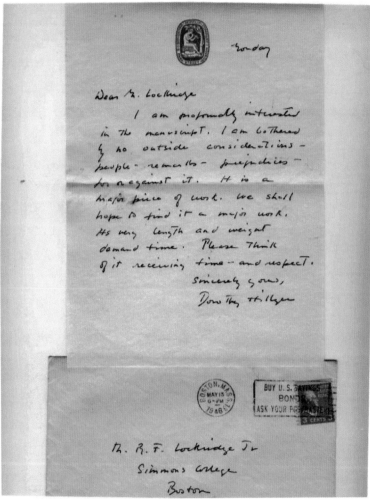

Houghton-Mifflin Editor Dorothy Hillyer writes Dad regarding her reading-in-progress of the twenty-pound manuscript he had submitted over the transom. He was in suspense regarding its fate and with a complete unknown's sense of entitlement had demanded a speedy response.

"Monday (May 13, 1946)

Dear Mr. Lockridge,

I am profoundly interested in the manuscript. I am bothered by no outside considerations--people--remarks--prejudices--for or against it. It is a major piece of work. We shall hope to find it a major work. Its very length and weight demand time. Please think of it receiving time--and respect.

Sincerely yours,
Dorothy Hillyer"

During the publication process she would become his surrogate mother and Paul Brooks, Houghton-Mifflin's Editor-in-Chief, his surrogate father. In the end, Dad felt deeply betrayed by them both.

IX

"THAT GREAT AMERICAN NOVEL"
Dorothy Hillyer, Senior Editor

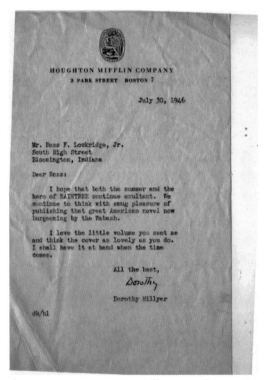

"The little volume you sent me": an elegant red-covered album consisting largely of photographs I had snapped of my father posing on the banks of the Eel River and in the river itself-- *Raintree County's* fictional "Shawmucky"--which meanders through the old Lockridge homestead and farm near Peru, Indiana. Dad elaborately produced the album, embellishing it with text from *Raintree County* and pencil drawings, for Houghton-Mifflin's publicity department which decided that snapshots of some backwoods clodhopper tramping around some obscure mud hole would not sell books.

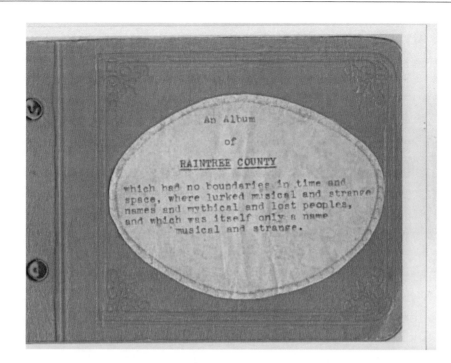

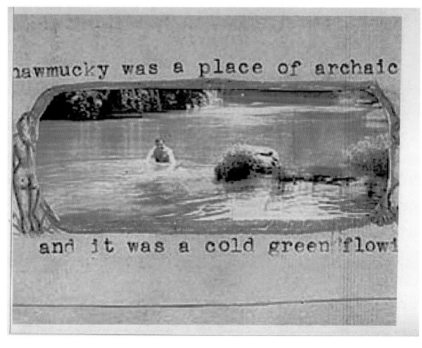

X

WINNER TAKE NOTHING

"If you have to change it, it wasn't worth writing in the first place." Mickey Spillaine

"The Universe does not care about the individual human being," my father writes in his March 6, 1948 *Suicide Note*. Neither did his beloved and trusted Publisher. Houghton-Mifflin saved my father a trek to the Post Office, but it cost him dearly.   Their   mere   mailing-in   of   the   M.G.M.   Prize "Applications" provided them the excuse to award themselves (in addition to the generous pot of M.G.M. gold to the "winning publisher") a literary agent's percentage--$250,000 in 2010 dollars—confiscated from Dad's prize-money. My father, who had lived on a shoestring his entire life, protested angrily--and futilely.

It was this cynical, high-handed act of thievery that precipitated his "breakdown."

Dad's Federal Income Tax Bracket was a whopping 90 percent--no "income averaging," no "loopholes" for The Hero of Raintree County, who had a wife and four small children, no job, no other source of income, and now no remaining inner resources and thus no hope of writing further novels given the emotional Inferno into which he had plunged.

He could only conclude that his publisher's true estimation of *Raintree County* was far lower than they had led him to believe.   Arm-twisting demands for extensive revision that followed the M.G.M. Award (and R.C's singularly lukewarm selection by The Book-of-the-Month Club*) underlined this grim conclusion, and left him wondering just whose novel was this "revised" tattered book into which he had sunk all his hopes and dreams?

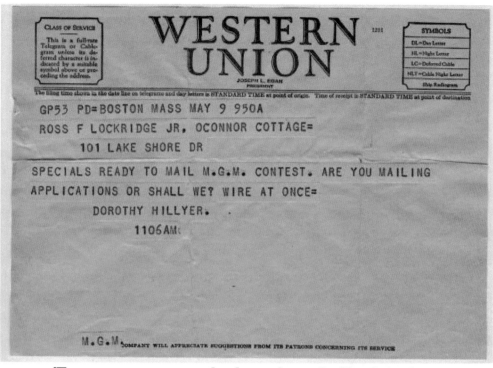

(To save money, we had no phone in Manistee)

At least my exhausted, demoralized father still had the moxie to fight off the eleemosynary proposition the bigwig bullies made him, that he wash his weary hands of his novel and relinquish it into the manicured paws of "a sensitive young editor we can all vouch for" for a complete rewrite--a free-gratis** revamping of the novel stem to stern, narrowing its focus and cutting it down by half.

How on earth could a novel vulnerable to seemingly infinite revision be worth a tinker's damn?

As Ernest Hemingway wrote to F. Scott Fitzgerald, "That terrible mood of depression of whether it's any good or not is what is known as The Artist's Reward."

"The Artist's Reward" is the sole reward my father accepted in the end.

*The Book-of-the-Month Club Editorial Board's Head Honcho, the iconic and universally distinguished Henry Seidel Canby, his three-pronged name a fixture in American households to this very day, said this of the January, 1948 Main Selection: "There may be more classical, more profound novels [than Raintree County] written this year, but certainly none more remarkable." Translating this into the American Language: "Though Raintree County may not rank among all the Truly Great American Novels of 1948 [!], it is, nevertheless, a sufficiently fascinating Freak Show to tide us over until THE BIG FISHERMAN swaggers into view."

**"free-gratis"?? On second thought, unlikely given the publisher's track record. More likely the financial muscle men of H-M, B.O.M.C. and M.G. M. would have yanked the fat fee of said "sensitive" editor right out of Dad's paycheck. And granted the guy co-authorship to boot.

XI

"THOSE RICH LOCKRIDGES"
A neighbor

A week or so after Dad's suicide Mom was waiting at the Bus Stop at the foot of South Stull Avenue to take the green Leppert Bus downtown for a nickel when one of our neighbors joined her and remarked, "That house up there? It's where those rich Lockridges live." He apologized profusely after my mother had introduced herself. The Kaiser was gone, Mom had never learned to drive, and we were by no means "rich."

Suicide was a lousy publicity move. "Inspirational" literature by a suicide smells like 3-day-old fish, and book sales dropped off into a swamp of rumination about "why he did it."

1948 Federal Estate Tax confiscated 50 percent of what remained after The Internal Revenue Service confiscated its own 90 percent. After the spondulicks dried up, after the depredations of publishers, attorneys, and taxmen, a paltry fraction of the *Raintree County* "fortune" remained for the probate judge to portion out thusly: 1/3 to my mother, 2/3 to the four offspring, requiring Mom to petition the Court regarding any and all increases in household and child-raising expenses.

The M.G.M. prize was payment-in-full for all movie rights. Lockridges get naught from the 1957 movie's all-too-numerous late-night airings.

XII

PROUD PARENTS

Shortly After Their Son's Suicide

The book is not *Raintree County*. Nor is it one of the numerous books authored--with my father's extensive collaboration, beginning in his teens--by Grandpa. *The Adventures of Perrine* was likely plucked at random from among the eclectic scores upon scores of volumes attracting coal-dust on the ragged yellowing book shelves of Murmuring Maples.

"Manifold and hideous the deeds which [he] scarce [hides] from men's revolted eyes. If any one despairs it should be I who loved him once, and now must live with him till God in pity call for him or me." **The Cenci**

Grandma's look says it all.

XIII

"ONE OF THE NOBLE"

Dad inscribed *Raintree County* to his mother, 5 weeks before killing himself.

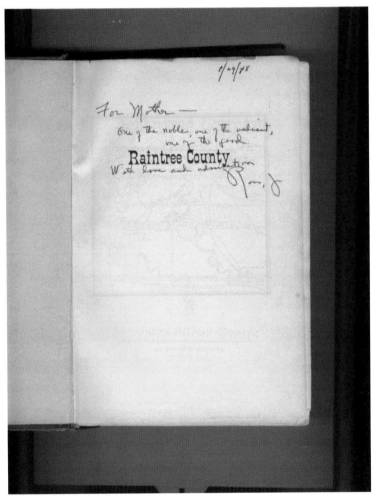

"1/29/48

For Mother--
  One of the noble, one of the valiant,
      one of the good.

**With love and admiration
Ross, Jr"**

Dad and Grandma, Dad's Indiana University Graduation, Spring 1935. The Well House (right) was a popular destination for marriage proposals.

XIV

THOSE WHO LEARN NOTHING FROM THE PAST
CONDEMN OTHERS TO REPEAT IT

My mother idolized Ross Lockridge, Sr., my grandfather.

After I complained about him, my Grandma Lockridge remained the one loving presence of my childhood.

Grandma had, of course, loved my father when she embroiled him in a pact that was anything but "noble," "valiant," or "good."

Old habits die hard, and following Dad's suicide I was "next up."

Niagara Falls, Sunday, July 24, 1949

**Ernest Lockridge (10), between
Grandma and Grandpa Lockridge**

XV

"JUNIOR"

When Dad learned that the British edition would strip the "Jr." (sobriquet of ridicule on the opposite side of the pond) from his name, he was, my mother told me, "beside himself" that anyone might think his novel was written by his father. Published by Macdonald, this edition did not appear until 1949; so, happily, my father did not live to see it.

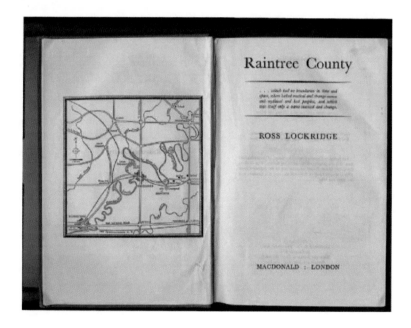

XVI

"THE DOG DID NOT BARK IN THE NIGHT"

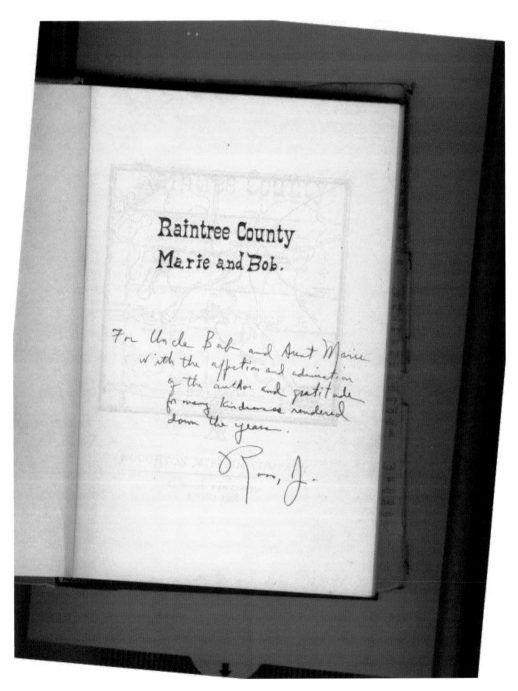

Raintree County
Marie and Bob.

For Uncle Bob and Aunt Marie
with the affection and admiration
of the author and gratitude
for many kindnesses rendered
down the years.

Ross, Jr.

"For Uncle Bob and Aunt Marie
with the admiration and affection
of the author and gratitude
for many kindnesses
rendered down the years.
Ross, Jr."

Dad was generous to a fault with inscribed presentation copies of *Raintree County* to aunts, uncles, in-laws and the like.

BUT

HE INSCRIBED NOTHING OF THE SORT TO HIS FATHER:

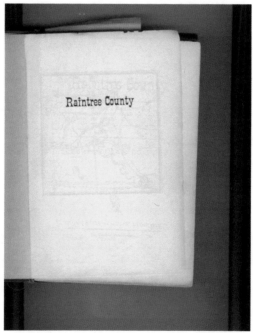

Inscription Page--Ross Lockridge Sr.'s copy of his son's best-selling novel.

"THE SADDEST EYES"

Of this photograph, a forensic psychologist remarked to me, "Those are the saddest eyes I have ever seen."

XVIII

"POETS ARE BORN SO" Suicide Note

John Wesley Shockley 1839-1907

A.K.A. "JOHN WICKLLIFF SHAWNESSY"

"There is nothing that we are than is not taught us."
Suicide Note

Elsie Shockley Lockridge worshiped her father, John Wesley Shockley (1839-1907), schoolmaster of a tiny Indiana farming community, and poetaster with Delusions of Grandeur that one day he would compose America's *Aeneid*! He looked like a poet--sort of. In his daughter's eyes her father's tragedy, and heroic distinction, lay in never having consummated his Quest. For whatever reason--dreams too noble for mere words? a materialistic 19th-Century unworthy of his Genius? "laying waste [his] powers" in a one-room shanty instructing generations of perspiring unwashed rubes?--he left behind a few scraps of derivative, escapist verse, but nary an Epic syllable. John Wesley Shockley died 7 years before my father was born.

While my father was little more than an infant his mother commenced indoctrinating him to hero-worship this backwoods Demigod. You have to be carefully taught, and the sooner the start, the more certain the result. Begriming a tabula rasa trumps the uncertainties of brainwashing.

Hoosier Schoolmaster--1893

John Wesley Shockley (front right), my great grandfather, age 54. Great Uncle Ernest Vivian Shockley, 15, my namesake, who died at 36 of pneumonia (front left); behind him, my grandmother Elsie Lillian Shockley, 13. Straughn, Indiana Schoolhouse, late spring, 1893, 14 years before JWS's death in 1907.

"Heroic Dreamer"

XIX

NOT ELIZABETH TAYLOR

SUSANNA DUKE (1844-77)

Impregnated out of wedlock at 15 by John Wesley Shockley, the real-life model for "Hero of Raintree County." They married but soon divorced, and Mr. Shockley's son vanished from his life.

Susanna Duke is a "real-life model" for *Raintree County*'s beautiful, mysterious, soiled, insane Susanna Drake, who thinks herself contaminated with "Black Blood."

The all-important "model," however, is Dad, himself, whose sense of his own unredeemable contamination provides the foundation of her character.

Chewing scenery like an old pro, the twentyish Elizabeth Taylor played the novel's Susanna Drake in the 1957 M.G.M. melodrama, "Raintree County," one of the lousiest movies ever to besmirch the Silver Screen.

STARS IN MY EYES

"M.G.M's 'Raintree County' *begins in tedium and ends in Apathy."* Time Magazine

Montgomery Clift and Ross Lockridge, Jr.'s kids

Summer, 1956, on location in Danville, Kentucky, where M.G.M. was filming the "Indiana" scenes of "Raintree County." The 4 children of Ross Lockridge, Jr., (that's me in back) pose with a miserably hung over Montgomery Clift in the role of Johnny Shawnessy, "The Hero of Raintree County."

Clift was known in Hollywood's gay circles as "The Princess Tiny-Meat."

The Crew Table where I chowed down was a smorgasbord of irreverence regarding the "real" Raintree County. Married to some old phony who'd sired her two children, Liz was getting lavish bouquets daily from one Mike Todd. A barbershop quartet of muscle-men with oiled torsos positioned the massive 70mm movie camera, lead-lined to muffle its racket; their real job, however, was providing stud-service to the Stars. Nice work if you can get it, except that even muscle-men were fungible, like light bulbs. An M.G.M. Star peremptorily ordered one of them discharged, an oiled torso with which she was having loud bouts of sex in her trailer. She'd wearied of him and wanted him gone--completely. The crew was grumbling about the shabby treatment of one of their own.

The top two Stars were in terrible physical shape. Liz was suffering a severe bout of bursitis. Two months earlier, May 12, 1956, whilst driving away drunk from a party held at Liz's Hollywood mansion, Monty smashed his Jag into a tree, fracturing his jaw, nose, and sinuses, and lacerating and partially paralyzing his face. Liz saved him from choking to death on a tooth lodged in his windpipe. Plastic surgery left him looking like a corpse. He spent the remaining 10 years of his life committing slow suicide.

Everyone should have the great good fortune to experience an unfiltered close-up of extreme fame.

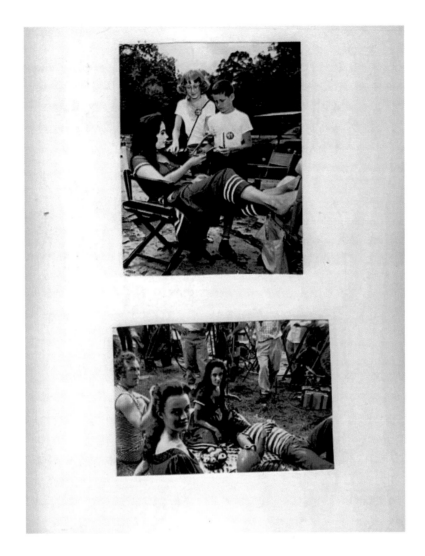

Top: The *real* Elizabeth Taylor, signing autographs for Jeanne Lockridge and Ross Lockridge III. Bottom: Liz and Monty, along with fellow-Hoosiers Nigel Patrick, a British ham, and the 1953 Miss Universe first runner-up portraying a mid-19th-century rural Indiana housewife. In take after take the hungover Liz and Monty flubbed their unmemorable lines.

My mortified mother destroyed my vivid 35mm Kodachrome slides of Monty goosing Liz in and out of a muddy pond. Mom had failed to preview the slideshow before presenting it to Bloomington's genteel "Conversation Club," where founding member Grandma Lockridge was in the audience.

During the uninhibited horseplay between The World's Top Two Motion-Picture Stars of 1956, Ross III had shouted, "Mom, is that acting?" and Liz shouted back, "Honey, you ain't seen nuthin' yet!"

Mom (right) was the inspiration for "Nell Gaither," the good-girl heroine of the novel. Eva Marie Saint (left) portrayed Nell in the movie. Here they are at the October 2, 1957 Louisville World Premiere of M.G.M.'s "Raintree County." Ms. Saint apologized to us for the movie, which she considered a dismal travesty of the book.

Before the curtain went up, M.G.M. star Russ Tamblyn shouted, "Hey, wouldja believe they flew me all the way out here without bringing me a date?" The 3 ½ hour premiere ended with a feeble scattering of applause from an audience that included M.G.M. luminaries Van Johnson and Jane Powell!

Exiting up the aisle, a small hairy fellow named Michael Todd, Elizabeth Taylor's current husband, was growling to his perspiring, miserably unhappy-looking wife, "It's your movie! It's your movie! It's your movie!"

At the Reception I got to shake the tiny moist hand of Happy Chandler, Governor of Kentucky. Also Van Johnson's, and miniature Jane Powell's. Tamblyn was laying siege to one of my cousins. The whites of Van Johnson's eyes were rabbit-eye pink.

XXI

"HOORAY FOR HOLLYWOOD!"

My parents photographed--November 25, 1947--touring the M.G.M studios after the M.G.M Prize ordeal and 13 weeks before Dad killed himself.

My smiling father is suicidally depressed.

XXII

BACK HOME AGAIN IN INDIANA (1948)

M.G.M. prize money bought this house to the ground while my parents were touring Hollywood. Mom's sister Clona, bank-teller extraordinaire, saw the Stull Avenue house going for a bargain-basement price, and Dad green-lighted the purchase sight unseen—blindly returning to the spawning ground to die.

The homeowners' son had just begun a lengthy sentence in the Indiana Pen for a hit-and-run homicide, driving drunk after the ceremony where he'd been named Bloomington High School's Athlete-of-the-Year. The *Bloomington Herald-Tribune* simultaneously featured both accomplishments on Page One, before the killer had been identified. Now his mortified parents were heading for the hills.

We moved into our new home on January 4, 1948, the same day my thrice electro-shocked father was released as "recovered" from Methodist Hospital of Indiana. Our new home was one mile from Murmuring Maples. Dad measured the distance with the Kaiser.

Our full-basement nestled inside a seamless limestone bathtub with no drain. Rain generated a wall-to-wall pond, and phalanxes of thumb-sized water bugs audibly scuttled up the concrete-block walls. My sole shot at gassing them with a Bug Bomb misfired in nightmare fashion with a writhing escalator of anthracite in death-throes mounting the basement steps and undulating in waves over the first floor. We obtained a dehumidifier on wheels and made peace with survivors and successive generations.

XXIII

THE PAW PAW LOCKRIDGE
FAMILY REUNION OF 1947

"Pie was the prize for these Hoosier literary cousins, Mary Jane Ward [Dad's double-second-cousin], author of 'The Snake Pit,' and Ross Lockridge Jr. (right), author of 'Raintree County,' at the reunion of the Lockridge family [in the Paw Paw Methodist Church] near Peru, Ind., yesterday. They are receiving their awards from Lockridge's father, Ross Lockridge, Sr., head of the Hoosier Historical Institute." (*Indianapolis Star*, September 21, 1947)

Grandpa was pressuring Dad to publicize the Hoosier Historical Institute, which explains its mention in the news story. Grandpa would have exerted no such pressure on Mary Jane, whose fame was tainted by her very public ties to mental illness: already her highly acclaimed 1946 best-selling novel was bringing about shakeups in the Nation's mental health system.

It still puzzles me that although Mary Jane knew my father was in terrible psychological straits, she did nothing to help him.

XXIV

CANARY IN THE MINE

To wit, Dad's 399-page epic poem, *The Dream of the Flesh of Iron*, the bulk of which consists of that most contemporary of American verse forms, the Spenserian Stanza. The poem constitutes a Chimera: *The Waste Land* and *John Brown's Body* mount *The Faerie Queene*. Its "Argument"? Here followeth Dad's version of The Eternal Triangle refracted through the Prism of Herr Freud. 1) "The Dreamer," 2)"The Beautiful One" versus 3)"The Boss," who is *"the objectified symbol of antagonism to the Beautiful One and thus also to the Dreamer or the soul of humanity. [The Boss] is, variously, lust, tyranny, [and] evil."* (Ross Lockridge, Jr., "Introduction") For *"The Dreamer or the soul of humanity,"* read *Ross, Jr.* For "The Beautiful One," *Grandma*. And, for *"the objectified symbol of antagonism . . . [of] lust, tyranny [and] evil,"* "The Boss," read *Ross Sr*. Here's a (typical, alas!) taste:

> *The Boss was with her, stood, and smiled at her.*
> *He glowed with confidence, removed his coat,*
> *The great soft coat of wool, expensive weave.*
> *His little pigeyes were red with lechergloat.*
> *He wiped his glistening forehead with his sleeve.*
> *I heard the ugly words he said to her. . .*
> *The Boss bent over and grabbed her slender waist.*
> *She fought. He crushed her body to the wall.*
> *His heavy muscles bulged. His face was tense.*
> *He panted hard. His body seemed immense*
> *Against her beauty and her slenderness.*

"The Dreamer" cranked out his never-published Oedipal Odyssey during 1939-40, down in the coal cellar of Murmuring Maples, whilst high up in the Sun Room "The Boss" was churning out a stupendous *oeuvre* of his own, a novel (now gone with the wind) concerning a pair of Native American lovers (one male, the other a distinctly masculine female) who learn in the end that they were kidnapped at birth by the "Redskins" who raised them, and are in fact, uh, WHITE! At the close of each writing day the companionable competitors, Dreamer and Boss, would serve up--to a) one another, b) The Beautiful One, c) Dad's older sister Teeter, d) Mom, plus e) a literarily insentient yrs. truly—their creative output fresh from the Ovens of the Muse. Dad's "subtext" flew well below The Boss's radar but (wink, wink) scored a bull's-eye on the receptors of The Beautiful One. Sharing a Secret Code was among the pleasures of a degrading pact wherein Son shielded Mother from defilement by assuming her position.

To save a buck we had moved out of the little log cabin wherein I was conceived, but despite the heady creative environment my mother loathed the indignities of Murmuring Maples where Teeter and The Beautiful One treated her like a small child.

Having returned, or regressed, to his childhood home, Dad required a "Flesh of Iron" as protective armor in that genteel hellhole of denial and abuse.

Any old father can be a *"Huge Imago"* to the son, but Grandpa was *Super-Sized!* In an autobiographical fragment which Dad wrote just before his death, he observes, "*This father [Ross, Sr.] was to the boy [Ross, Jr.] a creature of almost terrifying energy.*"

My father bats out *The Dream of the Flesh of Iron* in the coal
cellar of Murmuring Maples. Research materials consist of *Life
Magazine.* The *"dream"* is a 399-page *nightmare. "Depressives
build dungeons in the air."* (Old Saying)

XXV

BLOOMINGTON DUO
MAKE HEAP BIG SPLASH

Lord of the Fly

On January 1, 1948 Professor *Alfred C. Kinsey*, Bloomingtonian and founder of Indiana University's Kinsey Institute for Sexual Research, came out with *Sexual Behavior of the Human* Male (a.k.a., "The Kinsey Report"), which topped the best-seller list for nonfiction simultaneously with *Raintree County* topping the list for fiction.

"The Kinsey Report" is fiction in science-drag.

The Institute during the years that Kinsey himself was in charge has become infamous for: junk science; sexual predation and staff orgies in the name of "research"; heavy reliance on the testimony of convicts, rapists, and sexual psychopaths; willful disregard of sampling techniques and statistical methodology; proselytizing a Religion of Polymorphous Perversity--to name some of the Institute's less egregious shortcomings.

Kinsey, himself a closeted homosexual and self-mutilating masochist, would have granted Ross Sr. high standing among pedophiles, whom he judged to be intrepid sexual pioneers.

Inclusion in Kinsey's Pantheon of Pedophiles would have heartened Grandpa, whose literary preference ran to little bands of men-without-women, societies unto themselves slogging in close-knit company through the Uncharted Wilderness. Grandpa wrote a couple of such adventure stories--a book for boys extolling LaSalle, and one extolling George Rogers Clark.

Unlike Freud, Kinsey did not deny the existence of incestuous child sexual abuse; he merely denied that it harmed anyone.

Expanding upon the Master, Kinsey's wingman and our next-house-over neighbor Dr. Wardell Baxter Pomeroy said, "In father-daughter incest, the daughter's age makes all the difference in the world. The older she is, the likelier it is that the experience will be a positive one. The best sort of incest of all, surprisingly enough, is that between a son and a mother who is educating him sexually and then encourages him to go out with girls."

Kinsey welcomed the contributions of pedophiles as Participant-Observers. "A number of persons have turned in sexual calendars and diaries showing their day to day activities over some period of time. They admirably supplement the information routinely obtained on the standard histories. In each of two cases there are over a thousand pages of such supplementary material."

We now know that these "two cases"--one (Rex King) a Middle-Western rapist of some 800 young children; the other (Dr. Fritz von Balluseck) a Nazi serial rapist-murderer of children who began corresponding with Kinsey from Hitler's Germany--pursued their prey while also providing Kinsey with the admirable "supplementary material" detailing their ongoing activities.

Kinsey urges his readers to follow in Von Balluseck's and King's path-finding footsteps: "Persons who have kept records or who are willing to begin keeping day by day calendars showing the frequencies and the sources of their sexual outlet, are urged to place the accumulated data at our disposal."

A predatory-athletic sexual Conquistador, Rex King was on a lifelong polymorphous-perverse Grail Quest to engage in the widest possible range of sexual intercourse in Human History: infants, children of either sex, ditto adults; corpses; goats, sheep, dogs, any of the "lower" mammals he could wrestle to a standstill; chickens; reptiles; road kill; the bulk of his immediate and extended family including one of his grandmothers; ad libitum, ad infinitum. *Ad nauseam.*

Nazi field-researcher Von Balluseck gave his little research subjects a choice between rape and the gas chamber.

I'm happy to report that however its scientific methods may have grown more sophisticated over the generations, the old Kinsey Ethos remains tenaciously intact. "Trained observer" Rex King lives on as the Kinsey Pantheon's Super Hero. A recent Institute Director enlightened a puzzled interviewer by patiently explaining the spasms and convulsions noted by Rex King when detailing his sexual intercourse with infants and small children of both sexes as simply "a matter of fit. The orifices were tiny; whereas, the genitalia of Rex King were *massive*!"

Dr. Kinsey--petty tyrant, closeted deviant, mad idealist with a Divine Right to follow his God-given appetites wherever they might lead--is Grandpa's "double, [his] brother." (Baudelaire, *Flowers of Evil*)

XXVI

GOODBYE, BLOOMINGTON

During the late 1940's and early 50's when I was a kid in Bloomington, Indiana, Kinsey's right-hand man Wardell Pomeroy, Ph.D., resided across the road from us in a miniature one-story limestone cottage where I hobnobbed with his three kids. I could never quite grow accustomed to Dr. Pomeroy's apelike nakedness. A coarse blanket of hair concealed his genitals as he padded about his miniature Castle. Matronly and kind, Mrs. Pomeroy arrayed herself, like my mother, in modest housedresses.

We little playmates enjoyed a jolly old time, though I'd scram whenever one of them would chirp, "Hey Ern! Mom and Dad are having sexual intercourse! Wanna watch?!"

Prudish and slightly scared, I only glanced at the various pedagogical devices Dr. Pomeroy ferried home from the Institute—such as, 52 cards, 52 positions.

I resisted Dr. Pomeroy's badgering to take my sexual "History," but did let him take me on a tour through the Skunk Works's newly renovated spaces which included a glass coffin or fish tank on struts, wires sprouting from all over. Couples were soon to be observed, filmed and "electrically measured inside there while engaging in sexual intercourse."

Dr. Pomeroy explained that much of the Kinsey Library was currently held hostage by one Arthur Summerfield, the U.S. Postmaster General. A hypocritical prude, Summerfield had a secret room where he pored over confiscated illicit treasures. When finally liberated, they would elevate The Kinsey Library to *Penultimatum* in terms of sexually explicit materials. The Vatican Library would—by virtue of its trove of off-limits paintings by DaVinci, Michelangelo, Raphael—forever retain its world-title: *Ultimatum*!

Stuffed with junk our cramped one-car garage gloomed beside our back alley like the Black Hole of Calcutta. From its maw I could see Kinsey's extended family funnel into the Pomeroy's cramped limestone cottage. Big Kinsey and all the little kinseys from bottom to top congregated for what I learned much later were orgies at which Kinsey required attendance to raise staff awareness, destroy inhibitions, and deepen research-sensitivity. Light-years ahead of staid mid-century Middle-Western couture, Clyde Martin's wife would come in Hot Pants, her spectacularly long, elegant legs untrammeled—indelibly etched in my mind's eye.

Ah, Bloomington! Peyton Place was Sunday School compared with Thee!

XXVII

ROSS LOCKRIDGE, JR., AND FAMILY

The Illinois Central Train Station at 17th St. and N. College Ave. Departing Bloomington for Harvard--1940

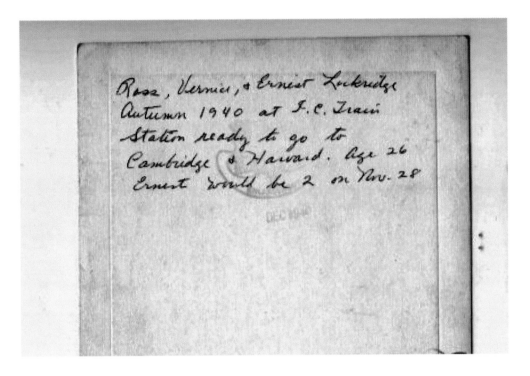

My mother's handwriting on the back of the photograph.

XXVIII

THE PHANTOM OF *RAINTREE COUNTY*

"This soul hath been/Alone on a wide wide sea:/So lonely 'twas, that God himself /Scarce seemed there to be."
Samuel Taylor Coleridge

"God is man's desire that good have an absolute guarantee. Once man became aware of death, learned anticipation, acquired knowledge, God became necessary as the guarantor of good, as the promise that made human life possible and tolerable." Suicide Note

Next page: the man I remember during his last weeks of life wandering like a zombie around our new house, or in bed staring hollow-eyed at the ceiling in our downstairs guestroom.

Following his suicide our mother encouraged us kids to remember him as a Superior Being whose Spirit was hovering over us everywhere. For me, his Ectoplasm's refuge and dwelling was the Garage where he "passed away." I visualized my father's Spirit wafting free of his carcass like car exhaust pooling at the roof's dark crevice.

XXIX

SNAKE PIT

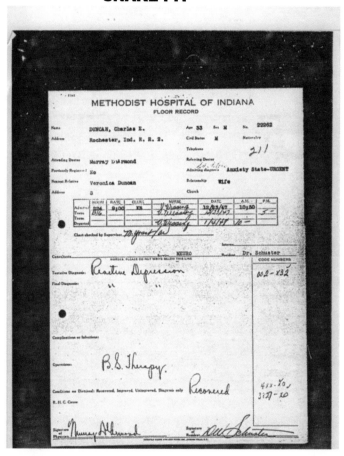

Herewith, a few of Dad's medical records from his short stint at The Methodist Hospital of Indiana, 12/23/47-1/4/48.

"Referring Doctor" is "Robt. Peters" (his signature), prominent Indianapolis physician, childless cross-dresser, collector of soft pornography and husband of Dad's paternal Aunt Marie. (cf. inscribed *Raintree County*, above). "Doctor Bob" thought so highly of Dad he had offered to send him through medical school if Dad agreed to join Doctor Bob's wealthy practice.

Struggling for Dad's soul, Mom appealed to "Doctor Bob" for help.

Her antagonist was Grandma, who had an A.B. in psychology (*Phi Beta Kappa*, of course) from Indiana University, but who opposed any and all psychological treatment for my father! No psychologists! No psychiatrists! Whatever her "good" reason for this weird self-contradiction, the *real* reason was terror that my father might spill the beans. Instead, Grandma was aggressively pushing a regimen of Mary Baker Eddy, whose philosophy--that the material world of space and time, the entire "real world" in which all human experience occurs, is only a malevolent illusion—had long been her balm and her salvation.

Dr. Peters facilitated Dad's admission to the psych ward of Methodist Hospital of Indiana. Hospital records show the good doctor present at the three Electro Shock Treatments administered by Dr. DeArmond ("EST & grand mal"--from "Nurses Clinical Record," 12-27-47, 12-30-47 and 1-1-48, "Dr. Peters here").

There is no record of psychotherapy. Dad reveals nothing about himself, not even his real name, having registered under the pseudonym "Charles E. Duncan." DeArmond learns nothing of Dad's real life, including that he is author of the current National Best-Seller *Raintree County*. An iron curtain of secrecy makes "talk therapy" impossible. Grandma and Grandpa could take solace that their boy remained such a good boy.

"Treatment" is limited to insulin, "Seconal etc.", plus Electro Shock Therapy "& grand mal." The "Nurse's Clinical Record" for 1-3-48 reads, "Cheerful and responsive. Wants to go home."

In fact, having been traumatically shocked as a child changing a bulb at Murmuring Maples, Dad had a deep-seated electrocution phobia. Mom said the unsedated Shock Treatments were agony for him. Dad claimed that he never lost consciousness during the *grand mal* seizures. It was *The Snake Pit* of Mary Jane Ward's bestseller.

Dad cranked up the charm, and as with all his endeavors he met with stellar success. After a meager two weeks in the hospital, three shocks treatments "to grand mal," a bunch of barbiturates, and no talk-therapy, he is discharged as "Recovered."

"12-23-47   2pm

Is unwilling to submit to a history and physical untill [sic] he consults Dr. DeArmond.
          R.M.Seibel

In September 1947 the patient had a 'let down' in which he was aware of a change in his feeling. He says it seemed as if he had lost contact with the world although this does not appear to be a process of depersonalization. There has been a tendency to avoid social contacts and he fears and dreads to face the ordinary daily problems. He has lost some weight, appetite has been below par, sleep poor and disturbed by harassing dreams.

Past illnesses have been insignificant.

[Physical Examination] reveals a well-developed, well nourished male who has no complaints except he doesn't know what has happened to him. Neurological examination--normal. Heart normal. [Blood Pressure] 120/74. Psychiatric examination shows good insight--no evidence of hallucinations or delusions. He is fearful, depressed, has lost confidence and feels helpless to straighten himself out.

Impression:
Reactive depression.
M.DeArmond"

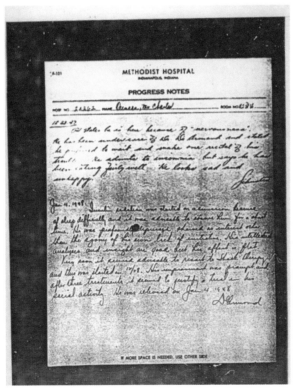

"12-23-47
[Patient] states he is here because of "nervousness." He has been under care of Dr. DeArmond and states he preferred to wait and make one recital of his troubles. He admits to insomnia but says he has been eating fairly well. He looks sad and unhappy. Schuster"

"Jan 4, 1948

"Insulin sedation was started on admission because of sleep difficulty and it was advisable to observe him for a short time. He was profoundly depressed, showed no interest other than the agony of his own lack of initiative. His intellectual analysis and insight are good but his affect is flat.

"Very soon it seemed advisable to resort to Shock Therapy and this was started on 12/28. His improvement was prompt and after three treatments it seemed to justify a trial in his social activity. He was released on
Jan. 4, 1948.
    DeArmond"

"*Dr. Peters here*"--signature cigarette in hand

Robert Peters, M.D.

Robert Peters, M.D. (L.) died of emphysema at 61. A chain smoker, "Doctor Bob" routinely prescribed cigarettes to calm his patients' nerves. He prescribed cigarettes for Grandpa who embraced tobacco with gusto.

Happy New Year!
January 1, 1948

"9:00 [a.m.] E[lectro]S[hock]T[herapy] [to] grand mal reaction [adm] by Dr. DeArmond"

XXX

HERE'S THE RUB

Dad once held an acolyte's faith that Sigmund Freud was the Open-Sesame to the human psyche. Indeed, my father once boasted that *Raintree County* would be *"the first-ever novel to do justice to Freud!"* So, why in the throes of his agony did Dad settle for a plain-vanilla therapist like Dr. DeArmond, in a primitive snake pit of Seconal and *grand mal* seizures? Why no Freudian Analysis? Or Freudian *Anything*? He had undergone Electro Shock Therapy, numerous *seances* with a Christian Science Practitioner, his father's vigorous ministrations--but there exists no evidence that he considered even a single consult with a Freudian Analyst. Why not?

Because like Virginia Woolf--sexually abused for 14 years by her much older half-brothers, the Duckworth boys--Dad was aware of Freud's final solution to the whole problematic issue of childhood sexual abuse. To rescue himself and his career from outraged attack, the fiendishly ingenious Freud invented the malevolent whimsy that "childhood sexual abuse" is nothing more than wish-fulfillment fantasy on the part of the so-called "victims."

Indeed, it was merely *reading* Freud that drove Virginia Woolf over the edge. Seeking clarity regarding her chronic depression, she was instead plunged into a "whirlpool" of confusion. "She hoped Freud would make some sense of her world, but Freud only convinced her that her memories were a fantasy, and that she was indeed mad. Virginia felt no hope. She could not face another relapse and ended her life." (Lee Marsh)

XXXI

SUICIDE CLAUSE

"15 April 1948

Memo To: Mr. Robert E. Neff

Mr. A.W. Scott, representing the Lincoln National Life Insurance Company, is interested in seeing the record of Mr. Charles E. Duncan, who was admitted under my care Dec. 23, 1947. At the suggestion and request of the family this name was used for Ross. F. Lockridge, Jr. Mr. Scott has Mrs. Lockridge's permission and mine to examine the record.

Murray DeArmond md"

The Bloomington, Indiana coroner was swift to rule Dad's death "*Suicide*," but life-insurance adjusters wanted to nail it down in order to pay out nothing in death benefits. The issue had been muddied by "Teeter," Dad's prison-matron older sister, who deep-sixed the Electrolux tube in the back-alley garbage can of Lockridge Family Secrets. My mother withheld this tidbit for 40 years. She did confide during my teens how Grandma and Teeter had dismissed her dire warnings about Dad, and how vindicated she felt by the coroner's ruling.

Whether Mom considered the vindication adequate exchange for receiving nothing from Dad's insurance policies purchased from her brother-in-law, I don't recall.

My mother gladly let my father's psychiatric records be handed over to insurance investigators. She wanted no uncertainty regarding Cause of Death.

As "winner," Mom--like her recently deceased spouse--took nothing.

XXXII

"CAN'T I BE YOUR GIRL?"

Miss Lillian Lockridge, Dad's older sister
A.K.A. "Teeter," "Aunt Kiki"
Matron, Indiana Prison for Women

When I was 14, Aunt Lillian--the formidable "Teeter"-- pressed her mouth to my ear and whispered, "Ernest, am I your girl? Just because I'm your aunt, can't I also be your girl?"

The Hoosier Historical Institute had died with Grandpa,

but Grandma persisted in grooming me to devote my life to her Father. *Raintree County*, heftier than most Bibles, had proven itself insufficient. Heaven forbid that Great Grandfather Shockley's one-gospel legacy remain outdone by Jesus Christ's four!

My interest in neither project was enthusiastic and not long before her 1961 death from a stroke even Grandma had run out of steam.

XXXIII

FATE IS CHARACTER

"Fate, which is simply man's inability to escape himself, played at its unselfconscious, sinister game, weaving its patterns around the little brownshingled house where the street made a corner and the cartracks bent. [Fate] was weaving a web in which it would lurk like a big black spider, poised to spring."

Ross Lockridge, Jr., *"Autobiographical Fragment,"*
February-March, 1948

XXXIV

DEATH WARRANT

"Life is useless, all useless." Ecclesiastes
"He must be wicked to deserve such pain."
Robert Browning

Ultimate Philosophy

Let no one blame another one. A man is an accumulation of many men, of all mankind quartered in a now, inescapable, unasked for, absolute, ultimate. Good and Bad are human discoveries. The universe is neither good nor bad. It does not care about the individual human being. It is he who learns care and who is taught good and bad from infancy. There is nothing that we are that is not taught us by our bodies, ## ### by events, by other men. #### God is #human's desire that good has an absolute guarantee. Once man became aware of death, learned anticipation, acquired knowledge, God became necessary as the guarantor of good, as the promise that made human life possible and tolerable. And thus there are good people, though whether they are good ### for reasons other than the compulsions of their experience or not, remains unanswerable. As for the evil, as for those who lose their grasp on the stuff of life, who become unable to cope with their world, are they to blame or are they not also the victims of long circumstance?

As for the miracle of being—it is of course a miracle, but it is not necessarily a good miracle. Some lives are fortunate, and some which seem fortunate ### become involved in agony, and who shall say whether this is through their own fault or not? Just as poets are born so, the brave are born so, and the cowardly are born so. That is, they are born to their fate. No one blames the child of less than ten for the errors of his personality, but link by link he is bound to the grown man.

"ULTIMATE PHILOSOPHY

"Let no one blame another one. A man is an accumulation of many men, of all mankind quartered in a now, inescapable, unasked for, absolute, ultimate. Good and bad are human discoveries. The universe is neither good nor bad. It does not care about the individual human being. It is he who learns care and who is taught good and bad from infancy. There is nothing that we are that is not taught us by our bodies, by events, by other men. God is man's desire that good have an absolute guarantee. Once man became aware of death, learned anticipation, acquired knowledge, God became necessary as the guarantor of good, as the promise that made human life possible and tolerable. And thus there are good people, though whether they are good for reasons other than the compulsions of their experience or not, remains unanswerable. As for the evil, as for those who lose their grasp on the stuff of life, who become unable to cope with their world, are they to blame or are they not also the victims of long circumstance?

"As for the miracle of being--it is of course a miracle, but it is not necessarily a good miracle. Some lives are fortunate, and some which seem fortunate become involved in agony, and who shall say whether this is through their own fault or not? Just as poets are born so, the brave are born so, and the cowardly are born so. That is, they are born to their fate. No one blames the child of less than ten for the errors of his personality, but link by link he is bound to the grown man."

[Ross Lockridge Jr., March 6, 1948]

The morning after Dad's suicide, while Mom was in our living room breaking Dad's collection of Stephen Foster 78's, I came across my father's Execution Decree on his desk in the guest room.

The dysgraphia in the lower left-hand corner is yrs. truly's ["I'm out at the car"], as are the blazing six guns. Uncle Shockley was all set to spirit me off in his Buick to Indianapolis where I'd stay until the funeral.

I may have dodged a bullet. Plenty of suicides far less philosophically grounded in Nihilism than my father have taken great pains to spare the wife and kids the "not necessarily good miracle" of continuing to live.

"Burningly it came to me all at once,
"This is the place!" Robert Browning

Canto 13 : Harpies in the Forest of the Suicides

XXXV

"AS FOR THE EVIL"

Our edition of Dante's DIVINE COMEDY, with engravings by Gustave Dore, was *the* Coffee-Table Book of my childhood. Fascinated with the haunting images of the *Inferno*, I repeatedly badgered my father to explain them. Here Dante, himself, "explains" HARPIES IN THE FOREST OF THE SUICIDES:

> *When the maddened soul forsakes its body*
> *From which it has removed itself by force,*
> *Minos consigns it to the seventh ring.*
> *It falls into the wood, without design,*
> *Dropping wherever chance may hurl it down.*
> *There like a grain of seed, it germinates.*
> *It grows into a sapling, then a tree;*
> *And now the Harpies feeding on its leaves*
> *Give pain.*   **(Tr. Lawrence Grant White)**

Dore's engraving shadows forth the Grail at the dead-end of my father's "glorious quest." Suicides seeding a twisted forest with their "maddened souls" are the dark-water reflection of the Johnny Appleseed of Dad's novel sowing Raintree County with seeds of the Golden Raintree. The randomly scattered souls of self-murderers growing "into a sapling, then a tree" with "Harpies feeding on its leaves" and giving "pain" represent the completion of my father's Quest for "the Sacred Tree of Life," a Quest which ends in the Inferno, "In *Raintree County*." (Cf. "Song of *Raintree County*," lyrics by Paul Francis Webster)

This familiar image of "mute despair, a suicidal throng" may have been among the last to flicker through my father's dying brain.

XXXVI

"GIVE UP HOPE ALL YE WHO ENTER HERE" *Inferno*

Spring, 1958

**Garage in which, 10 years earlier, Dad had died. I'm holding
our beloved rescue cat, Powder Puff.**

XXXVII

MY FATHER'S MUSE

"So young to go under the obscure, cold, rotting, wormy ground!" Beatrice, *The Cenci*

Beatrice Cenci (1577-99) mere Hours before her Beheading

The Condemned portrayed as though through her Executioner's eyes

A reproduction of Beatrice Cenci's death-house portrait (Guido Reni, 1599) adorned the living room wall of our Boston apartment during the years that my father was writing *Raintree County*.

Beatrice paid with her head for arranging the murder of her domineering, incestuous father. Pope Clement VIII refused to pardon Beatrice because he "[held] it of most dangerous example in aught to weaken the paternal power, being, as 'twere, the shadow of his own." (Shelley)

In addition, Count Cenci--a blood-thirsty monster of depravity, but a most wealthy one--"had during his life repeatedly bought his pardon from the Pope for capital crimes of the most enormous and unspeakable kind. The Pope probably thought that whoever killed the Count Cenci deprived his treasury of a certain and copious source of revenue." (Shelley)

Back in the day, however, any old Patriarchal Head of Household could get away with murder and worse where family members were concerned. And his victims had no recourse.

Imagine that!

Shelley wrote *The Cenci* "as a light to make apparent some of the most dark and secret caverns of the human heart." Dad embellished his copy's margins with his indecipherable shorthand.

Beatrice Cenci's pitiable shade haunted our cramped Boston apartment during the years my father was Gatling-gunning *Raintree County* through the old Royal. At first, I believed that she was Grandma as a young woman, but Mom said, "No, not that," and Beatrice settled into a puzzling shadow on our living room wall, no blood relative but just another victim of injustice who lived an agonizing life and died an agonizing death.

Beatrice's executioner suffered the agonies of the damned. My father forestalled any such consequences by executing himself.

XXXVIII

"A NOVEL WHICH . . . MIGHT REALLY MERIT THE TITLE OF 'THE GREAT AMERICAN NOVEL'"

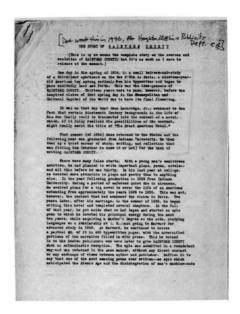

Following Houghton-Mifflin's acceptance of *Raintree County* in 1946, my father gave their publicity department the lengthy, detailed "Story" of how it came to be.

"One day in the spring of 1934," it begins, "a nineteen-year-old American boy sprang suddenly from his typewriter and began to pace excitedly back and forth. This was the idea-genesis of *Raintree County* . . . It was on that day [in Paris] that Ross Lockridge, Jr., awakened to the fact that certain Nineteenth Century backgrounds in the life of his own family could be transmuted into the content of a novel, which, if it fully realized the possibilities of its content, might really merit the title of 'The Great American Novel.'"

But this account fails to mention the feverish journal, a 58-page aesthetic manifesto, into which the "nineteen-year-old American boy" in Paris then proceeded to pour out his *"plan"* to write "The Great American Novel."

XXXIX

"WRITE THE GREATEST SINGLE PIECE OF LITERATURE EVER COMPOSED"
Ross Lockridge, Jr., Paris--1934

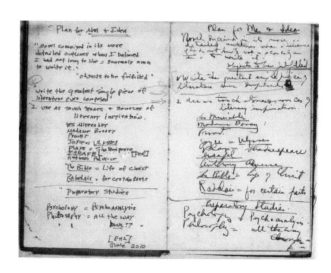

"Plan for Man & Idea

Novel conceived in its more detailed outlines when I believed I had not long to live=scarcely even to write it.

Objects to be fulfilled

Write the greatest single piece of literature ever composed.

2. Use as touch stones and sources of literary inspiration.

> **Les Miserables**
> **Madame Bovary**
> **Proust**
> **Joyce=Ulysses**
> **Plays=Shakespeare**
> **Israfel [Poe]**
> **Anthony Adverse**
> **The Bible=Life of Christ**
> **Rabelais=for certain parts**
> > **Preparatory Studies**

Psychology=Psychoanalysis
Philosophy=All the way back"

Thus p. 1 of the *Journal* which Ross Jr., not yet out of his teens, flooded with ideas for the novel that became *Raintree County*. By p. 50 he is writing that "the first object of my return [from Paris to Bloomington] shall be the complete mastery of the English language to the end that my use of the language be the most brilliant ever known."

"The greatest single piece of literature ever composed"--?

The Iliad and Odyssey? Genesis? The Divine Comedy?Hamlet? Paradise Lost? The Canterbury Tales? Ode to a Nightingale? War and Peace? Middlemarch? Madam Bovary? Great Expectations? The Brothers K.? Ulysses? The Search for Lost Time?

This grandiosity--the outward mask of defilement, deep grieving, and despair--fueled my father's life's work from beginning to end and made his collapse virtually inevitable.

It is not possible to exaggerate the extent to which my father derived his identity and self-worth from the writing of "the greatest single piece of literature ever composed," so that when the process ended and he saw the product to be not "that good" (and how could *any* new work of literature hope to be "*that good*"?), he had nothing left, having bet his life on the turn of a single card.

Though such grandiose ambitions might be seen as "normal" for a teenager, they sustained my father through his 20's, and into his 30's until his spirit finally cracked.

And why, at 19 and in robust health, did my father write that he had "not long to live?" *Death* was seldom far from his mind, as borne out in an autobiographical fragment written just before he died:

"Always after [Rossie] had visited Lindenwood Cemetery and had followed the winding drives to the place where his brother [Bruce] was buried, the boy loved cemeteries. Nothing else seemed to him so quiet, lovely, peaceful, and so full of the meaning of human life as these places of death. An indefinable longing filled his heart when he stood in these places where the ground was full of stones with letters on them. Lindenwood Cemetery-- beautiful Lindenwood."

XL

ISRAFEL

*"And the angel Israfel hath the sweetest voice of
All God's creatures."*   Holy Koran

In Heaven a spirit doth dwell
Whose heart-strings are a lute—
None sing so wild—so well
As the angel Israfel—
And the giddy stars are mute.
...
If I did dwell where Israfel
Hath dwelt, and he where I,
He would not sing one half as well—
One half as passionately,
And a stormier note than this would swell
From my lyre within the sky.

Edgar Allan Poe

That my father sneaks tiny "Israfel" into his short-list of
(otherwise) gargantuan "touch stones" shines the searchlight
on the vastness of his literary ambition.

Why, he might out-sing *even Grandpa Shockley*!--and claim
solely unto himself The Beautiful One's undivided love.

XLI

DOUBLE WHAMMY

"A house divided cannot stand itself."
Pere Nabri

Throughout his life my father struggled to forge an identity separate from the man whose name he bore and whose mission was to obliterate him. Senior bullied Junior to be his amanuensis, ghost-writer, office-boy, Boy Friday--and . . . well, *worse!* Grandpa relentlessly dogged Dad to take on an array of "projects," as though he were a gifted vassal, an exotic parrot or trained monkey. When Dad emerged from the Asylum with all his defenses gone, Grandpa came to the rescue. He put Dad on display in Rotary-Club-type venues where his inanition disappointed the micro-audiences. Hoping to "revive" my father, Grandpa challenged him to a memorization contest after "EST & grand mal" had disabled his phenomenal memory. Grandpa resumed badgering Dad to assume co-directorship of The Hoosier Historical Institute.

If Grandpa could not save Dad, neither could the enormous success of *Raintree County*, a work inspired by his mother and written "*for*" her. Dad had rebelled against his father only to deliver himself into his mother's strait-jacket.

Trapped in a nightmare marriage to an *incestuous homosexual pedophile* (talk about hitting the trifecta!), Elsie Shockley Lockridge co-opted her brilliant youngest son to transform the sow's ear of her degraded existence into the silk purse of The Great American Novel.

In the Civil War between his parents, Dad took on the role of his mother's Savior, sacrificing himself to make her the victor.

March 6, 1948: Gutted and cannibalized upon the family hearth, my father finished off what little remained.

XLII

NOT PICKING UP THE TORCH

Grandpa proceeded to train me in public speaking--or, in projecting my voice from the barn to the rear of the house, reciting passages he had me memorize: e.g., "How They Brought the Good News from Ghent to Aix," "Concord Bridge," "The Gettysburg Address," "The Boy Stood on the Burning Deck," "Charge of the Light Brigade," "Little Orphant Annie." Grandpa was indoctrinating me in the lore, minutia, and "manly virtues" necessary to someone who might one day qualify to direct The Hoosier Historical Institute when I ungratefully called a halt.

Meanwhile, Grandma was extolling the superhuman virtues of her saintly father, far more sensitive and romantic than her brutish spouse."Ernest," she confided following Grandpa's death, "when your grandfather came courting, my father warned me, 'Elsie, your young man's bright little eyes reflect a shallow soul.'" Great Grandfather Shockley had been "reborn" in my father, and Grandma sensed that it was I who now embodied both of these dead souls, "heroic dreamers" whose greatness lay not in what they did but in what they dreamed.

Not unlike most victims of intolerable childhood abuse Dad went somewhere inside his head for escape, and it became a way of life.

XLIII

PARENTS FROM THE NETHER REGION

1940

XLIV

GRANDIOSITY

My father took grandiosity to its extreme. *Raintree County* was to be the greatest single work of literature ever composed in the best writing ever. This ambition had a foundation of sorts, a sandy one, in a) unnumbered first-place finishes of his Indiana youth, including Indiana State Championships in typing and shorthand; b) while in his teens he is already ghosting and/or co-writing his father's mediocre but published books; c) Grandma gives him an I.Q. test which confirms--objectively!--her long-held certitude that Dad possessed the brains to be her father's Avatar; d) Dad's academic record remains the highest in the history of Indiana University (he was known, half-humorously, as "A-Plus Lockridge"); e) he receives the top scores in the Sorbonne's foreign-exchange program.

His Indiana University M.A. Thesis: *Byron and Napoleon.*

In place of a mere suicide note he leaves behind an *"Ultimate Philosophy."*

He crucifies himself at Christ's age, 33.

XLV

ELSIE SHOCKLEY [LOCKRIDGE]

Disciple of Mary Baker Eddy who preached: *"There is no life, truth, intelligence, nor substance in Matter. Spirit is immortal Truth; Matter is mortal error."*

Age 21

Honeymooners and "Friend"--July, 1902

XLVI

RAMPAGE

The day after Grandma's death, my Uncle Shockley literally ripped his way through her steamer-trunk of memorabilia, focusing special attention upon her and his father. While "Uncle Shock" was taking a break, I seized the opportunity to retrieve from the trunk's damp bottom a couple of rotting packets, Dad's letters home from Paris (1932-3) and Boston (1940-1946), the bulk of them written to his mother.

March 7, 1948, the morning I learned my father was dead, my mother packed me off to Indianapolis to stay with Uncle Shockley while funeral arrangements were underway.

 A couple of days later driving me back to Bloomington where my father's corpse lay on display surrounded by gardenias in our living room, Uncle Shockley advised, "Ernest, you may not actually feel sad, but by golly you had sure better *act* as though you do!"

XLVII

"THE COMPULSION OF EXPERIENCE"
Suicide Note

In his coffin my father's hand was cold and hard as dry ice. Food weighed down our kitchen table. I took a mouthful of pineapple pie, and it made me sick. I now loathe pineapple pie. The stench of gardenias nauseates me.

 Displaying the wisdom that typified them in all matters of significance, the elder Lockridges determined it to be in everyone's best interests that I *not* attend my father's funeral. I spent that day alone wandering the wooded acreage of Murmuring Maples and carving rings around the trunks of saplings, using a pearl-handled pen-knife with the legend, "WIN THE WAR."

Slaughtering trees.

 Daring God to punish me.

Uncle Shockley

XLVIII

SUICIDE SURVIVORS

Early spring, 1948, our side yard is a chaotic nest of crabgrass. Ross Lockridge, Jr.'s widow and children a couple of weeks after Dad's death. I'm the one acting sad.

XLVIX

"LO! I AM WITH YOU ALWAYS."

1953

The Death-Car went back to the Kaiser-Frazier dealer.

A haunting shadow, the *death-house* remained.

Gas Chamber de-commissioned into playground equipment.

Childhood's Mausoleum.

XLX

HEAR NO EVIL, SEE NO EVIL, SPEAK NO EVIL

With four young children depending on her, and the instinct of blind trust when the greatest vigilance is called for, my youngster of a mother was vulnerable to financial "schemes." A Sunday school teacher of mine sold her the fantastic notion that there was a fortune to be made raising chinchillas in the home!

For $20,000 early-1950's dollars delivered unto my Sunday school teacher for the actual animals, plus additional pelf for cages and "essential" paraphernalia, Mom adopted four brace of chinchillas. The ark was provided by her older brother Leon who moved in next door with his family to do the dirty work, which continued through the '50's with additional thousands bleeding from my mother before it grew undeniable that that the "cornucopia" was a sucking black hole.

The little beasts tore one another to shreds. *We* were expected to kill and skin them! There had never been a market for "home-raised" pelts. The Sunday school teacher had long since absconded to Florida.

Meanwhile, the Family Lawyer talked Mom into investing in some dingy downtown Bloomington cafeteria (which he co-owned) that returned pennies in profit.

At the Family Lawyer's urging, she financed the home mortgage of some stranger who couldn't qualify for a bank loan.

Her Bloomington Stock Broker tied her up in a failing restaurant chain.

By the time my mother remarried, 16 years after my father's suicide, she was nearly destitute.

L

THINK NO EVIL

Soon after Grandpa died, my mother approached me with a proposition. Would I mind going out to McCormick's Creek State Park with one Oscar Tharpe ("OT") "who wanted to get to know [me]." OT had called my mother, and she consulted Grandma who said it was "All right"so long as I "watched out for [myself]." They wanted to avoid "hurting OT's feelings." They told me OT was "harmless." This sounded frightening, but who was I?

A flabby old bald guy, OT had his hands all over me in the Park's swimming pool. We had hamburgers at a drive-in in Elletsville while OT chattered away about "Morals." When OT called for our last date, I told my mother, "No!" but she made me agree to go out with OT again because she did not want "to hurt OT's feelings" and besides OT was "harmless." So I said ok if my best friend Jack came along. In the Princess Theater, pal that I was I made certain that Jack occupied the seat of honor betwixt OT and me. Throughout the movie OT had his hands all over Jack, who kept fighting him off. OT insisted on dropping Jack off first. Then OT took me to his house where he went on and on about what a terrible person Jack was and I should not consider him my true friend. "Get rid of that guy Jack," OT said. "Jack is no friend of yours!" In OT's living room was a photo of a much younger OT with hair and a dewy-eyed poetic gaze.

OT

Later, I learned that OT had been prowling after boys for decades, including--a generation ago—my own father, and that none other than Grandpa had told OT to "get lost." Grandpa knew exactly how "harmless" OT was. OT taught a boys-only Sunday school class on "Morals" at Bloomington's First Christian Church, where my parents had been married.

Every weekday afternoon following banking hours at the bank where OT was teller, he made tracks to the University High School locker room and hung out with whichever team of athletes happened to be disrobing.

LI

"MORALS"

a)The North American Man-Boy Love Association (NAMBLA) prides itself for providing high-level "Moral Instruction" to the little boys who are their prey; similarly,

b)Sociopaths of an academic stripe are drawn to the subject of "Morals" like stink on rice.

c)Grandpa was a sacred fount of Moral Instruction. The morning I was to begin 4th grade, Grandpa ordered me to stop seeing Wesley Anderson, my playmate that summer. Otherwise, Grandpa explained, "All the real boys are going to call you a ******-lover."

d)Grandpa found *Raintree County's* profanity and sexuality wounding to his moral sensibilities, and a public embarrassment. He was deeply disappointed in my father but decided that on balance the novel's literary merits perhaps outweighed, although they by no means justified, such crude violations of the high moral standards Grandpa had always endeavored to instill in his progeny.

Grandpa Holds Forth

LII

NOSTALGIA OF EMPTINESS

Raintree County is the *crie de coeur* of a mortally wounded spirit.

Months of non-stop revising to meet impossible demands by the Book-of-the-Month Club and M.G.M.; being swindled out of a fortune by a revered and trusted publisher; returning home to Bloomington to be shunned by the I.U. English Department where he'd achieved the highest undergraduate and graduate-student grade average in University history; being bludgeoned with a review by that Department's new Professor of Creative Writing (hired by Dad's ex thesis advisor) second in Sadism only to *The New Yorker's*; bidding farewell to the grand project that had sustained him since his teens, then concluding that *Raintree County* was "no good"; enduring the lethal ministrations of his dreadful parents: such stressors triggered the underlying pathology that fractured my father's sanity, much as influenza had ruptured--with fatal consequences—the encapsulated tubercle that Thomas Wolfe (*Raintree County's* chief literary influence) had contracted as a child growing up in his mother's boarding house for tuberculars.

Exhausted, beaten to a pulp, my father lost the strength to keep the Monster in its cave.

A nostalgia of emptiness pervades my father's novel, a phantasmagoric homesickness or longing for a non-existent past that enervates the soul, leaving both reader and author hollowed out. Six decades following publication *Raintree County* still possesses sufficient hypnotic force to drive the susceptible reader hysterical with nostalgia.

Attention must be paid to the fact that my father's life was one long *Peine Forte Et Dure*, and that in the end it required the adding-on of a not inconsiderable tonnage to crush his heart.

LIII

SKELETON IN THE CLOSET

CLOCKWISE FROM TOP LEFT: a) Family Patriarch Ross Franklin Lockridge, Sr. b) Grandma and newborn firstborn Bruce c) Bruce, shortly before his drowning d) Grandpa with Ross Jr. (3).

Grandma would recount how on the day before Bruce drowned he had challenged her to see who could hold their breath longer. "I see my Bruce down there holding out till the last possible moment!"--her soul-rich eyes glistening at the lovely coincidence of it all!

LIV

FAMOUS LAST WORDS?

Grandma actually surmised a "material-world," real-life connection between something Dad said on the afternoon of March 6, 1948, and his suicide that night. "If I'd only known what he meant, I might have changed his mind," she told me. But she refused to say what it was that he actually did say.

I've concluded that my father must have made reference to the Legendary Lockridge Double-Long Electrolux hose that Teeter pitched down the Burn-hole of History. Dad might well have "explained" himself to Grandma, using a dark, sardonic jest:

"Mother, we find ourselves sharing our South Stull property with an elephantine rodent who is simply trumpeting to be put out of his misery."

Grandma could not reveal this, because it also meant revealing the ugly, squalid "material" actuality of my father's suicide.

She wanted me to remain inside her bubble.

LV

MARY BAKER EDDY

If, as Mrs. Eddy teaches with utter certitude, "there is no life, truth, intelligence, nor substance in Matter"; and if the so-called "real world" of "sin, sickness and death" is merely error and illusion and therefore "unreal"; then it follows that the outrages perpetrated upon Grandma's sons, and their suffering and suicides and drunken self-destruction are mere Phantasm, the "mortal errors" of "Matter" as opposed to the "immortal truth" of "Spirit." What mother need worry overly much about, or protect her children against, non-existent horrors?

I read lengthy passages from Mrs. Eddy's *Science and Health* to Grandma on her deathbed at her request. It was like reading a fairy tale to put a child to sleep.

ELSIE SHOCKLEY LOCKRIDGE

Channeling Mrs. Eddy?

LVI

"LET NO ONE BLAME ANOTHER ONE"
(Suicide Note)

Each year when spring rolled 'round, Stella Hull--Grandma's age, quiet and unassuming, well-spoken, genteel to a fault, wearing a clean, threadbare dress, bringing her belongings in a single carpetbag—would visit Murmuring Maples for two weeks, sewing, darning, sweeping, cleaning, cooking, doing laundry, ironing, scrubbing floors, making the old homestead spick and span, "an' earn her board an' keep."

Born into "a distinguished Southern family," Stella eloped with "a handsome no-good" who drank himself to death, leaving his destitute young widow to survive as an itinerant "houseguest" and drudge. And yearly reminder of the fate of wives of Grandma's generation who lost their husbands.

STELLA

1898

LVII

"A PERSON APART"

"Never ask, 'Oh, why were things so much better in the old days?' It's not an intelligent question." Ecclesiastes

"Heaven has special care of me.'Tis plain I have been favored." Shelley's Count Cenci

Insanity

**Ross Lockridge, Sr.,
Indiana University Freshman**

"A PERSON APART": thus Ross Lockridge, Sr., characterizes his hero LaSalle--and himself.

In *LaSalle* (1931), a history for boys, Grandpa indicted an encomium--a veritable frenzy of self-love--that stands out as an exemplar of transparent Projection:

"He [LaSalle/Grandpa] may be characterized as an impossible dreamer who accomplished no real results, who only followed wild fancies that brought expense and trouble to others and suffering and tragedy to himself. Such is the lot of those men whom a mixture of great faults and great virtues lifts above the common sphere. Their passions betray them into errors.

"But in the softening light of time we begin to see the man in his true light. He seemed to feel convinced that he could not act otherwise than the way he did. [He] had a lofty vision based upon the highest patriotism and the purest religious motives [and] in all his work he never wavered, never relaxed his purpose, never lost his courage; and never abandoned his religious faith.

"He towered high above all hardships. The utmost that extreme disaster could do was to delay him; it could not defeat him or cause him to despair. He was to leave imprinted upon the pages of time the tragic but inspiring record of a glorious hero attempting the impossible, guided on by a gleam of hope like a Holy Grail."

The insufferable La Salle was assassinated by his tiny band of followers.

Grandpa's Holy Grail was to resurrect the Great American Past, installing its Heroes in a Pantheon within the collective American Psyche. Throughout my childhood Grandpa revealed this Gallery of Secular Saints to be populated not only with La Salle, George Rogers Clark, Lincoln, Little Turtle, Tonti, Tecumseh--an eclectic panoply of historic figures--but with fictional figures as well: Robinson Crusoe; Hawkeye (a.k.a. Natty Bumppo, Deerslayer); characters from *The White Company*; Grandpa's hero of the Silver Screen, Randolph Scott; Black Snake, eponymous hero of Grandpa's unpublished opus *Black Snake and White Rose.*

Grandma worshipped her dream-father, John Wesley Shockley, the Perfect Man, and badgered my father into becoming his Avatar. Grandpa worshipped an "impossible dreamer whose great virtues [lift] him above the common sphere," whose "passions" might "betray [him] into errors," but who remains a "glorious hero attempting the impossible": i.e., *GRANDPA HIMSELF*, "dauntless spirit" and seeker of the "Holy Grail"— Ross Franklin Lockridge, Sr., who relentlessly dogged my father to embody Him and to bear His Noble Flame.

Delusions of Grandeur, regressive fantasies, rape of body and mind: the mix-and-match pathologies of my father's dreadful parents mangled his spirit and plunged him into the Abyss.

LVIII

"GLORIOUS HERO"

"I please my senses as I list. I have no remorse and little fear, which are, I think, the checks of other men."
Count Cenci

Drawn and Quartered by his son, Shockley Lockridge

Grandpa's "great faults" operate on a plane with his "great virtues" to "lift him above the common sphere" and seal his greatness as a "mighty spirit" "guided by a gleam of hope like the Holy Grail."

Such a man "could not act otherwise than the way he did." He is but a pawn to his "passions" which are, nevertheless, morally balanced out by the tragedies that inevitably befall "a glorious hero attempting the impossible."

But aren't all such heroes victims of the very passions that fuel their "lofty vision" and drive them upward to Greatness? No wonder they expend their gargantuan energies upon fungible little inferiors such as, say, sons and grandsons placed on earth at their Sire's pleasure for His pleasure.

Not unlike the stalwart hero's outsized hunger for fame and food, His God-given, gargantuan Lust for Life grasps at yet another staple in the Visionary's Cupboard--both to fuel the magnificently impassioned Visionary, and to *relieve* him, allowing him to "[relax] his purpose" if only for a few cherished moments so that he might gain respite to recharge his mighty energies and continue onward and upward.

Who, then, would presume to deny the taste of human flesh to Alexander the Great? Julius Caesar? Dr. Kinsey? Rex King? *Ross Franklin Lockridge, Sr.?* Is it not the sacred duty of us nobodies to regard being subsumed into the very fabric of a Demigod as Life's Greatest Honor? Small wonder the "glorious hero" was baffled and outraged by my "*disobedient insolence.*"(Count Cenci)

Goya, "Saturn Devouring One Of His Sons"

"My children's blood I thirst to drink." Count Cenci

LIX

GRANDSON OF PALEFACE

When I awaken on the feather mattress in the Sun Room I pretend that I'm asleep but it never works. Grandpa's tiny alert eyes gleam like cockroaches. "Awake, Scuffie? Come here!" He lifts his comforter. His bare feet pinion my ankles. I fight his hands away. He stinks like a garbage can. "Don't you know what real men do in the woods, Scuffie? You're not one of those little sissy girls!"

My mother looks stricken. "You'd better be telling the truth, Ernest, is all I have to say."

Grandma and Teeter arrive at Stull Avenue right after supper. "Might be a good idea if Mother and I spoke with Ernest in private," says Teeter. She and Grandma share the Master Bedroom, while Grandpa is relegated to the Sun Room, which he shared with my father during elementary and high school.

"Would the front room be all right?" Mom asks.

"Come along, Ernest." Teeter edges sideways through the living room doorway. "Coming, Mother?"

I'm in a straight-backed kitchen chair, facing Teeter and Grandma on the couch.

Am I in for it now! Oh Boy!

Teeter says, "Ernest? This began how long ago?"

"Right after my father died."

"Does Dad touch your penis?" Teeter asks.

"Oh, Teeter!"

"Please, Mother. Allow me to get to the bottom of this in my own fashion."

"Only when I can't keep both his hands away at once."

"And what about *his* penis?"

"I won't touch it!"

"What about your bottom?" Teeter asks.

"Grandpa holds me down on my back."

Grandma is swaying and sighing.

"Now, Ernest, did Dad, I mean your grandfather ever have you take his penis in his mouth?"

"No!"

"Thank the Lord!" Grandma puts in.

"Think hard, now. Does your grandfather ever push his penis inside your bottom?"

I am nauseated.

"Any questions, Mother?"

"No, Teeter."

"Ernest, why have you only now decided to come forward with this?"

"Grandpa told me that he doesn't have forever."

"Well, that about covers it." Teeter rises heavily from the couch. "Mother and I are going to have a little talk with Dad. Mother?"

"Do I have to get in bed with Grandpa anymore?"

"No, you most assuredly do not! Come along, Mother."

We go into the hallway where Mom is standing.

"Ernest is going to be fine," Teeter assures her.

"I have always had only the highest regard for Ernest's grandfather," my mother tells them.

"Well, that's not to say Dad doesn't have his little peccadilloes," Teeter says.

"Teeter. I need to go."

"I need to know what this is all about," my mother says.

"Let me put it like this," Teeter says. "I don't mean to accuse Ernest of making a mountain out of a molehill but it's nothing that cannot be dealt with within the confines of the Family."

"Is Ernest telling the truth?" my mother asks.

"I'm not feeling well," Grandma says.

Teeter says, "Some things are best swept under the rug."

"Does Ernest require punishment?" my mother asks.

"Don't anyone even *dare* to punish this child!" Grandma cries out.

"Now, now, Mother. Come along. We're finished here."

LX

MOM

It was sheer serendipity that an itinerant photographer photographed Vernice Baker in the back yard of her childhood home the day before she married my father whom she worshiped and adored and who a decade later left her with four small children, but no last will and testament or note of farewell.

Mom, who had typed and retyped thousands of pages for my father and consecrated the last page with her tears, saw him dedicate the completed *Raintree County* to his *mother,* "for" whom he had written it.

Following 16 years of chaste widowhood, Mom also lucked out in her re-marriage, to Dad's M.A. thesis-advisor whose diabetes he controlled by controlling my mother and who during their 16 years of marriage never got around to including her in his will.

Vernice Baker

On the Day Before Her Marriage to my Father

For My Mother
ELSIE SHOCKLEY LOCKRIDGE
This book of lives, loves, and antiquities.

Dedication Page, *Raintree County*

LXI

"THE MAN WHO WASN'T THERE"
Edward Lear

"He hath ever but slenderly known himself."
King Lear

*"Some lives which seem fortunate become
involved in agony."* **Suicide Note**

Dad's friends and acquaintances described him as being the most charming, *secretive* person they ever met. They "never really knew him." Like Edwin Arlington Robinson's "Richard Cory," he was "a gentleman from sole to crown, clean favored, and imperially slim. And he glittered when he walked. We thought he was everything to make us wish that we were in his place. And Richard Cory went home and put a bullet through his head."

LXII

LITERATURE ABHORS A VACUUM

The family dynamics that gutted my father gutted his novel.

Johnny Shawnessy, "The Hero of Raintree County," reprises the role of "Dreamer or Soul of Humanity," the nameless protagonist of *The Dream of the Flesh of Iron*. But neither "Dreamer" becomes even a marginally realized flesh-and-blood human being. Shawnessy remains an Entity, a compendium of thoughts, feelings, and--above all--"Dreams," "floating like a vapor on the" novel's thousand-plus closely printed pages. Action never defines him; neither does what he says or how he says it. He neither rises, nor falls, to the level of everyone in, say, Dickens, Joyce, Hemingway, O'Connor, Faulkner.

The more he strives to become Everyman, the more my father becomes The Man Who Wasn't There. This ever-expanding emptiness constitutes *Raintree County*'s central flaw, and it is fatal. The man who knew my father least well was himself.

LXIII

"THE PROMISE THAT MADE HUMAN LIFE POSSIBLE
AND TOLERABLE"

In a childhood that was chaotic, violent and bewildering, my sustaining hope--despite my father's making it clear that I was too often a mere pest who got in the way of his frantic writing-- was that he loved me.

I like to believe that the following letter was written with love:

February 1, 1947

Dear Ernest,

Daddy has been very busy, and that's why you haven't had a
letter from me lately.

I thought you might want to know what's happening along
Mountfort Street. The other day I was walking to our building,
when suddenly a small boy shot out of an alley running with all
his might and two larger boys after him. On looking closely
at this boy, I saw that it was none other than our old friend
Henry Miller. I said, "Hello, Henry," and Henry immediately
began to walk under my arm, while the two bigger kids slunk off,
muttering things under ########### their breath. "How is the
William McKinley School these days, Henry?" I said. "It stinks,"
Henry said. "Who's your teacher now, Henry?" I asked. "Bucktoothed
Murphy," Henry said. "She stinks." "Is she hard on you, Henry?"
I asked. "She pulls your hair and hits your knuckles with a
ruler," Henry said.

Just then we saw a small blocky kid walking along the street
loaded with war equipment and having a surly smile on his face.
It was Lee Oliver, who hasn't grown much since you saw him last
probably because he drinks coffee. After Lee had passed, I said,

"Henry, does Lee still beat the boys up?" "Not so much now,"
Henry said. "The other kids can run faster now."

It wasn't many days after that, that I came out of our
apartment building and saw a small boy stirring with a stick
in a puddle of dirty slush right in front of the mailbox
in the gutter. It was Errol, who is bigger now but no better
looking. "What are you doing, Errol?" I asked. "Fixing it
so that cars will get stuck in this mud," Errol said.

Same old Errol.

All the kids want to be remembered to you, Ernest, and
Sandra Kelley promises me that she has some old comic books
that you may have. Don't get your hopes too high, though, as I
still don't have these comic books.

You can see that life on Mountfort Street is much as it
always was except that little Ernest Lockridge is no longer
dodging around corners there to get away from other kids. Some
relics and reminders of little Ernest Lockridge are still there,
however, as every now and then I see a terribly battered old gun
or something that looks like one you used to have.

Henry Miller says he knows where I can get caps, and I'm
going to try to get you some.

I hope you are getting along fine in that good school that
Grandma has started you at. You know that Daddy expects you to
be a good boy in school and at Grandma's. Thanks ever so much
for that good letter about the basketball game, and write me
again soon.

Love,
Daddy

February 1, 1947

Dear Ernest,

Daddy has been very busy, and that's why you haven't had a letter from me lately. I thought you might want to know what's happening along Mountfort Street. The other day I was walking to our building, when suddenly a small boy shot out of an alley running with all his might and two larger boys after him. On looking closely at this boy, I saw that it was none other than our old friend Henry Miller. I said, "Hello, Henry," and Henry immediately began to talk under my arm, while the two bigger kids slunk off, muttering things under their breath. "How is the William McKinley School these days, Henry?" I said. "It stinks," Henry said. "Who's your teacher now, Henry?" I asked. "Bucktoothed Murphy," Henry said. "She stinks." "Is she hard on you, Henry?" I asked. "She pulls your hair and hits your knuckles with a ruler," Henry said.

Just then we saw a small blocky kid walking along the street loaded with war equipment and having a surly smile on his face. It was Lee Oliver, who hasn't grown much since you saw him last probably because he drinks coffee. After Lee had passed, I said, "Henry, does Lee still beat the boys up?" "Not so much now," Henry said. "The other kids can run faster now."

It wasn't many days after that, that I came out of our apartment building and saw a small boy stirring with a stick in a puddle of dirty slush right in front of the mailbox in the gutter. It was Errol, who is bigger now but no better looking. "What are you doing, Errol?" I asked. "Fixing it so that cars will get stuck in this mud," Errol said.

Same old Errol.

All the kids want to be remembered to you, Ernest, and Sandra Kelley promises me that she has some old comic books that you may have. Don't get your hopes too high, though, as I still don't have these comic books.

You can see that life on Mountfort Street is much as it always was except that little Ernest Lockridge is no longer dodging around corners there to get away from other kids. Some relics and reminders of little Ernest Lockridge are still there, however, as every now and then I see a terribly battered old gun or something that looks like one you used to have.

Henry Miller says he knows where I can get caps, and I'm going to try to get you some.

I hope you are getting along fine in that good school that Grandma has started you at. You know that Daddy expects you to be a good boy in school and at Grandma's. Thanks ever so much for that good letter about the basketball game, and write me again soon.

       Love,

       Daddy

LXIV

"BORN TO THEIR FATE"

Second Grade, William McKinley School, Boston
1945

LEE OLIVER, top row, 2nd from left. HENRY MILLER, top row, 2nd from right. SANDRA KELLEY, middle row, far right. ERNEST LOCKRIDGE, seated, center. ERROL NEWTON (not pictured) was the younger son of our apartment building's alcoholic janitor, "Old Man" Newton, who mercilessly beat his kids. Dad and I saw him repeatedly kicking his eldest, Bucky, in the gut. I doubt Errol even attended a school.

LXV

BLESSING WELL-DISGUISED

Tough little LEE OLIVER, whose father had been shot dead by the Nazis, led a gang that pursued me for 3 years. Lee made me an offer to join his gang if I'd help beat up my best friend, Henry Miller, but I refused. Later, back in Bloomington I put an end to my Elm Heights classmates' taunting about my father's suicide by going after them with my fists. I had learned to enjoy fighting. All of this "training" came through when the time arrived to fight off Grandpa.

The "ruptured eardrums" that kept my father out of World War II were a mystery to me, until I realized their likely etiology lay in Grandpa's blows to our ears when subduing his little "Scuffies."

LXVI

SUNDAY SCHOOL

My junior high Sunday School Teacher (the chinchilla salesman came later)--Ed--was a married pedophile whose preference ran to the little girls in our Sunday School class. His pretty wife acted like it was really cute when Ed kissed and fondled them.

Our Junior Choir Director was a pedophile whose preference ran to the little choir girls.

Our married Senior Minister attacked my teenage cousin in the church office where she was volunteering. He absconded with a young Church Secretary to Champaign, Illinois, where one of our brother Congregations had invited him to set up shop.

Our Junior Minister, who styled his hair like Elvis, was discreetly discharged for engaging in sexual relations with numerous adult female members of our Congregation who came to him for marital counseling. He opened up a men's clothing store in Bloomington's first strip mall.

However heartening and instructive the resiliency of such people—as though the Universe exists to mirror back unto them their abiding love of themselves--my childhood blessed me with a raft of designer role models custom-made to hone an awareness of Evil.

LXVII

THE LORD OF THE FLIES

1946- LARRY ERNEST JEANNE (+PUCK)

Following our father's suicide the role of *de facto* father to my three siblings--5, 4 and 2--fell unto me. Over them like a vapor floated our flawless Father Which Art In Heaven, whilst down on sorrowful, earth-bound South Stull Avenue resided an all-too-solid and (at 9) inadequate little surrogate who nonetheless towered above his littermates like the Colossus. The resulting cocktail--prominent in the mix, an unchecked, stultifying unilateral sibling rivalry ginned up with a vicious Oedipal twist—has been poisonous.

LXVIII

NEST OF VIPERS

Easter, 1953

I threw myself into music, sports and drama, and read voraciously in the hope of becoming a novelist. I was an active member of The Boy Scouts and the Methodist Youth Fellowship. I collected stamps.

One sibling chose to pick up my self-same musical instrument, my major sport, and to follow my academic and intellectual interests--plus myriad other mimicries, little ones, big ones, dogging my footsteps and hoarding a bottomless reservoir of grievance.

Two siblings exhibited a taste for Biology.

One harvested road kill from the roadside, rotted away the flesh in rot-boxes, boiled the bones, wired together skeletons of squirrels, opossums, raccoons, moles, and mounted them on polished wooden planks, little Lazaruses raised from the tomb.

The other housed poisonous reptiles in cages in the bedroom, feeding them living mice at the outset, later freezing the mice solid in our freezer and thawing them as needed.

A quarrel erupted between the two fledgling biologists over who had dibs on a dead mule beside a country road. Mom drove them to the kill site but put her foot down at carting the festering mass home. To mollify their violent tantrum-throwing, she allowed them to take the maggoty head. Someone must have brought the Family Hatchet.

The massive skull moved restlessly about our house from room to room before settling at last on the storage-ledge of our garage.

LXIX

RAINTREE COUNTY: THE RELIGION

Both National Epic and Holy Writ, *Raintree County* has spawned a loopy little cult complete with 1) Bible (The Novel), 2)Hero (Johnny Shawnessy), 3) Martyr (Dad), 4)Paradise ("Raintree County which [has] no boundaries in time or space"), 5) True Believers, 6) "Vatican Library" wherein the Holy Holographs are stored, 7) Hagiography, 8) Apostates, 9) Unbelievers,10) Defilers.

Lockridges under various surnames are particularly vulnerable to the cult, inclusion in which confers a *faux* sense of entitlement, plus additional life-impeding toxins such as the obsession with seeing *Raintree County* declared--in the cult's fantasy of a Perfect World--"The Official Great American Novel."

The cult offers its literature free and postage paid. A hardbound hagiography of Dad, first edition, in mint condition, complete with dust jacket, costs not a farthing. And, one may choose between 1) a copy autographed by the book's author, or 2) a rare unautographed copy.

"Never Never Land" is fine and dandy, until a chronic disregard of common decency and truth renders the inmates dangerous.

LXX

"THERE ARE GOOD PEOPLE"

"God made us plain and simple, but we have made ourselves very complicated." Ecclesiastes

MY MOTHER'S FAMILY, THE BAKERS
Whose "stage of action" was the Real World

Hugh Baker, Beulah, Clona, Aubrey, Lily Baker & (seated) Baby Leon. 1909. My mother was born in 1914.

Father and Sons

Leon Baker, Hugh Baker, Aubrey Baker
1927

Grandma and Grandpa Baker

Visit to Murmuring Maples, 1939.
(2nd floor, left:
The Sun Room)

South Lincoln Street, Bloomington, Indiana

Hugh Baker, in his garden, Labor Day, 1938

"Only someone too stupid to find his way home would wear himself out with work." Ecclesiastes

LXXI

FROM THE DIARY OF HUGH BAKER (1874-1946)

"July 30, 1911

"To whom-so-ever may chance to read this diary I wish to say that these pages have been sadly neglected. Simply indifference, not business nor anything else has caused the neglect. However, I will write a few things that have come to pass since last we wrote in order to bridge over the chasm of time intervening. As about the first thing of importance after March 27, 1910 was the appearance of Halley's Comet. You will note that on April 23rd, 1910 Rufus Weinland, Osman Welch, Milt L. Borden and myself went fishing in White River near Gosport, Indiana. Halley's comet was plainly to be seen in the Eastern sky about (3) three o'clock in the morning.

"Halley's comet was a grand sight to behold. As it appears so very seldom I will not be permitted to look upon it during my present incarnation, but I trust that it will be the good fortune of my progeny to read these pages and when they are permitted to behold the famous tailed star they may recall hereby the name of their far distant ancestor who had the same privilege while on the stage of action. To that end my name is here inscribed.

Hugh Baker
1874-1911   yet living"

Grandpa Baker

Ernest Lockridge, artist--May 5, 1941

LXXII

"THE FUTURE OF AMERICAN LITERATURE"
(reviewer)

JANUARY 20, 1948. Basement of L.S. Ayres Department Store, Indianapolis, Indiana. Dad grits his teeth and puts on his game face preparatory to signing "the greatest single piece of literature ever composed." Having decided that *Raintree County* is a humiliating failure, he faces the public ordeal with dread exacerbated by a bad omen: during a January 7 attempt to make the 50-mile drive north from Bloomington to Indianapolis a rear wheel came loose from the Kaiser.

That's Mom at Dad's left shoulder. Scads of Hoosiers showed up to have their *Raintree County's* autographed. Dad affixed his signature to a stack of copies for L.S. Ayres to market later on.

Following his suicide, his widow purchased four of these for his children.

LXXIII

SIR ISAAC NEWTON'S THIRD LAW OF MOTION

*"Make way, make way for the Hero of Raintree County!
His victory is not in consummations but in quests!"
Raintree County*

*"Descend with me. This is the dream I dreamed."
The Dream of the Flesh of Iron*

"The poor son-of-a-bitch." The Great Gatsby

Grandiosity such as my father's does not arise from a heightened sense of self-worth but from its opposite, a profound sense of self-degradation, the conviction that his life is unfit to be lived.

Grandiosity offers an equal but opposite reaction to ongoing spiritual disintegration: "If only I achieve the Greatest Goal I can imagine, the Greatest Single Work Ever Written and in the Greatest Writing since the Human Race emerged from the muck, my Dream, my Holy Grail--who will call me 'worthless'?"

Suffocating in quicksand, he grasps for the mud-slick root.

It helps to be attractive, brilliant, in good health, to have a mother who nurtures and encourages you. In place of delivering you from Evil, however, the Beautiful One ushers you into her most intimate confidence and, spoon-feeding The Sacred Pabulum, initiates you into a mystical, mythical Secret Society of Two, then furnishes both the map to your Dream-Quest, and the very Grail to whose pursuit you must devote your life. This lifeline staves off drowning until you achieve your Dream, or give it your last best shot.

No matter how thickly you've whitewashed the sepulcher, however, that stench clogging your nostrils is *you!* Your strength gives out, your vision clears--or seems to--and reveals that you are not merely soiled, you, yourself, are *Evil*.

Further, you have exposed yourself as a fraud. The greater your bestseller's visibility, the greater your exposure to universal ridicule--now, and for the ages. Helplessly, you watch your bloated 1000-page punch line to a filthy joke buoyed to hideous Best-Sellerdom. Fame is your death blow. No refuge from universal calumny and derision exists for you now but in the grave.

"Any man must be unfortunate who has written so bad a [work of literature] that it is yet accessible to readers one hundred years later." (Ross Lockridge, Jr., *Byron and Napoleon*)

Your Grail-Quest nears its end as you join the throngs of the Damned, *"those who lose their grasp on the stuff of life, who become unable to cope with this world."*

The root slips from your grasp.

And descending forever into "the Dream [you] dreamed" you drown yourself in the Holy Grail of Suicide.

Rest in peace.

LOCKRIDGE

ROSS F. LOCKRIDGE Jr.
1914 — 1948

VERNICE BAKER
1914 — 1994

**"*Home is the sailor, home from the sea,
And the hunter, home from the hill.*"**
Robert Louis Stevenson

LXXIV

EXORCISM

"Better this present than a past like that."
Robert Browning

And my "Legacy"? Grief, anger, defiance, the knowledge that I counted for nothing in a universe that would have made no sense at all had I not also felt responsible. My bouts of childhood illness had worn my father out. The shortcomings that made him punish me severely had *literally disappointed him to death.* My mother's overwhelming grief left her nothing with which to reassure or comfort me. Plus, who should come to the rescue but Grandpa?

It took awhile to realize that Grandpa was one of those all-too-well-disguised blessings--our veritable Skeleton in the Closet, who unwittingly palmed me the key to the suicide of his youngest child.

With understanding comes reordering, chaos resolves into sense, which helps. I mean, it does. Really. Good thing my childhood "therapy" was emphatically of the self-help variety. They could have fobbed me off onto some Freudian.

I no longer blame my father for abandoning me to the wolves. Suicidal depression is like the guy who survives a head-on collision to find the white-hot engine-block flaming in his lap and he's begging the State Trooper to finish him off.

LXXV

"LINK BY LINK
HE IS BOUND TO THE GROWN MAN"

Murmuring Maples, May 20, 1939

Ross Lockridge, Jr., and Ernest Lockridge

LXXVI

IF NOT NOW, WHEN?

Not aging, or public exposure, or the guilty knowledge of adult family-members can stop with utter certainty the incestuous pedophile. Even in death he squats like a repulsive toad beneath the family tree, or a grotesque spider in its web surrounded by the sucked-dry husks of his descendents.

Why don't our "Protectors" bar the door? Call out the Cavalry? Shoot the bastard?

Rule One in the Survival Game is, "*Me first!*" The Big Bad Wolf isn't out there blowing your door down. You're his houseguest! His *vassal.* He's king of the castle. He makes the rules. He'll keep right on taking care of his family, just as long as everyone looks the other way when he gorges himself at the Family Trough, Saturn devouring his young.

Unlike my father I had a refuge--of sorts--from the domestic Minotaur whose "great faults and great virtues [lifted] him above the common sphere."

Those of us who have exposed an adult sexual abuser of children know well the great rewards that befall us. Moreover, we have experienced first-hand how these rewards multiply in direct proportion to our abuser's blood ties, how our family falls all over itself with gratitude: "Oh, see how your brave act has spared your small brothers, sisters, cousins, even the children of neighbors and strangers!

"Why, can it be that you've protected and spared little precious US? Oh, Thank you! Do please tell us--how can we ever thank you enough?"

Uh huh.

Younger siblings will claim "we were not abused"; therefore, you are lying, or delusional. Of course, child-molesters have techniques for using a child surreptitiously. And, a seasoned practitioner practices sufficient discretion and self-control to create a modicum of deniability, especially when past crimes are known to family members. One-at-a-time can be accused of "making up things," but two or more than two poses a problem. And, there's individual taste. Grandpa preferred us "less than ten," perhaps, but not by all that much.

But I stopped him in his tracks, at least within the narrow confines of my own litter. I did that--with the Amazonian support of Grandma and the formidable Teeter who treated his assaults on me as the last straw!

At great cost.

My mother worshiped Grandpa; my father's death only strengthened their bond. Not long after Dad's suicide, I had observed Mom and Grandpa in a passionate kiss, in our Stull Avenue living room, in the vexed presence of Teeter and The Beautiful One. Loathing her mother- and sister-in-law, my mother dismissed all of it as sheer rot. This included me.

Being branded "liar," "evil," and "insane" represents only a small portion of a reward that includes withdrawal of parental love and support, alienation from one's closest relatives (essential, ultimately, to survival), marginalization, ridicule, slander, and outright treachery. Bottom-feeders with no visible dog in the fight attack us. Sadistic thugs admonish us to "turn the other cheek." Those once "near and dear" all too generously disseminate the lie that we are demented, or deceased. No matter who we are or how impressive our accomplishments in life, we can expect to be grossly vilified:

Such is the universal tactic employed to discredit all adult survivors of childhood sexual abuse!

To hell with it! When challenged to swallow the contents of a spittoon and spit out something in your own defense, walk away. We know what we know.

And remember:

We are not alone! Too often it is we the Survivors who are one another's true sisters and brothers.

And:

There is no necessity for the evil perpetrated upon us to undo us.

Here is an Absolute Truth: The best revenge is *living well!*

And another: Anyone who imposes upon you *their* agenda for *your* life carries the *Black Death.*

You Molesters and Rapists of children: *you will be known.* Perhaps not until the world's been cleansed of your filthy presence, and in spite of your having outlived your victims and parceled out your boasting to Facilitating Institutions such as Kinsey's Skunk Works with their false promise of a hermitically-sealed vault for your exploits to rot and fester in the dark; and in spite, too, of misguided family closing rank to shield your vile acts. Even so, one day those vaults will crack and your Legacy will become your souls' nauseating stench fouling the nostrils of Humanity.

 At twice my father's age at his death, plus five, I want to set the record straight, in hope that wide knowledge and understanding of this American tragedy might help prevent the waste of even one life.

"SOME LIVES ARE FORTUNATE"

ERNEST LOCKRIDGE (b. Nov. 28, 1938) graduated Phi Beta Kappa with Honors from Indiana University in 1960. A Rhodes Scholarship finalist he was Woodrow Wilson and Lewis-Farmington Fellow at Yale University where he earned "Honors" in all his graduate classes, was awarded an inaugural Woodrow Wilson Dissertation Fellowship (1962-3) and completed his M.A. and Ph.D. in English within three years (1960-3). He was hired by Yale's Department of English (1963-71) and taught at Yale during the Golden Age when its English Department was internationally rated Number One. Lockridge was selected Fellow at The Center for Advanced Study, University of Illinois at Champaign-Urbana (1969-70). In May 1971, Yale's seven undergraduate literary prizes (including the never-before-awarded prize for Satire) were won by his students, with work written under his supervision. Lockridge is author of three novels, one of which, *Prince Elmo's Fire*, was a Book-of-the-Month Club selection. His *Twentieth-Century Interpretations of The Great Gatsby* (Prentice-Hall) went through 20 printings, remained in print for a quarter-century and continues to sell briskly over the Internet. All but one of his essays in literary criticism have been included in anthologies, and singled out for special praise. From 1971-91, Lockridge taught English at The Ohio State University where in 1976 he was promoted to Full Professor and in 1985 was awarded the university's premier award for teaching excellence, "The O.S.U. Alumni Award for Distinguished Teaching." In 1991, he took "early retirement" after 28 years in full academic regalia, and has devoted himself to writing, jazz sax and clarinet, painting, family, and travel. *Travels with Ernest* (Rowman & Littlefield Publishers), co-authored with his famous wife, sociologist and poet Laurel Richardson, was published in 2004. He delivered "The O.S.U. Department of English Fifth Annual Emeriti Lecture," April 8, 2010. Emeritus Professor of English, Ernest is a jazz musician and painter of award-winning paintings that have appeared in solo exhibits, galleries, and on the covers of books. He is father of three, stepfather of two, grandfather of eight.

This Book is Dedicated to

Children Everywhere

7570620R0

Made in the USA
Charleston, SC
19 March 2011